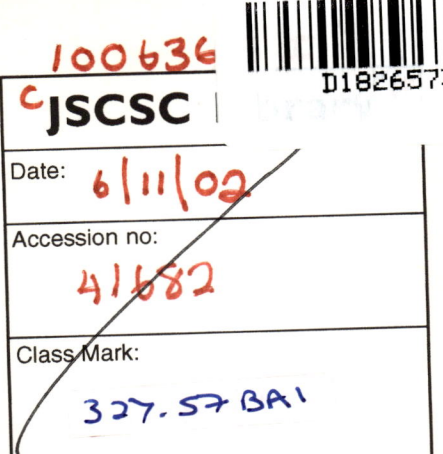

THE WORLD TODAY

Problems of Peace

BY GERALD BAILEY

formerly Director of the National Peace Council,
Lecturer in International Relations

Ginn and Company Ltd
18 Bedford Row, London WC1

F. W. Cheshire
Melbourne · Canberra · Sydney

Acknowledgements

We are grateful to the following for permission to use copyright photographs: Almay (p 55); Associated Press (pp 27, 54, 87); Camera Press (pp 9 top, 10, 64, 82 right, 89, 91); J. Allan Cash (p 48); Central Office of Information, Crown Copyright (p 42); Mary Evans Picture Library (p 97); FAO photo by F. Botts (p 131 bottom); Friends Peace and International Relations Committee (p 147); John Lewis Partnership (p 32 top); Mansell Collection (pp 6, 82 left, 97); Paolo Monti (*frontispiece*); Radio Times Hulton Picture Library (p 9 bottom); Trustees of the Imperial War Museum (pp 15, 19 left); United Nations (pp 32 bottom, 44, 72, 74, 105, 108 top, 111, 114, 120, 131 top, 135); United Press International (pp 75, 108 bottom, 135, 139); U.S. Air Force and Ministry of Defence (p 19 right); Voluntary Service Overseas (p 41). The diagrams and maps are based on material provided by *Africa*, *Insight*, *Scala* (Frankfurt), *Science Journal* and *United Nations*, for which we make grateful acknowledgement.

G. BAILEY 1970   107010   ISBN 0 602 21188 3
Published in Great Britain by Ginn and Company Ltd, London and in Australia
by F. W. Cheshire Publishing Pty Ltd, 346 St. Kilda Road, Melbourne, 3004.

Phototypeset by Oliver Burridge Filmsetting Limited, Crawley, Sussex
Printed in Great Britain by Butler & Tanner Ltd, Frome and London

Contents

1

War and peace

A personality of the B.B.C. radio programme *The Brains Trust* used a phrase which became a kind of theme song for him and almost invariably began his contributions to the discussion. 'It all depends what you mean,' he was accustomed to say, 'by such and such a word.' Definitions, he insisted, were all-important. Words were essential, of course, because without them no communication of ideas or opinions was possible. But unless there was some agreement as to the meaning of the terms used, discussion became confused and unprofitable.

To no word does this dictum of Dr Cyril Joad apply more aptly than *peace*. We assume peace to be desirable. We know that it embodies the hopes of all reasonable men and would not quarrel with the judgment of an earlier philosopher, Thomas Huxley, that it 'represents the end and purpose of all society'. We know further that in the age of nuclear weapons the search for world peace is the most vital of all searches because unless we find it, we may soon reach the end of human history.

But what, in fact, does the word mean today? What exactly are we searching for? What kind of peace are we talking about? Tacitus said of the Romans that 'they created a desert and called it peace.' Hitler brought a kind of peace to the smaller countries of Europe in 1940 when his armies overran their territories and took them forcibly out of the Second World War. His was the peace tyrannically imposed on free men, the peace of the iron heel and the prison camp. There are many other examples in history, recent and remote, in which peace has simply meant the enforced submission of a nation conquered by a stronger power.

The meaning of peace
There is no need to search for this kind of peace. It comes, unsought, all too readily. The peace we shall be looking for and talking about in this book cannot be defined in a single or a

simple phrase, nor can it be achieved dramatically at a given moment in time. It is more truly the expression of the peaceable human spirit and as we shall constantly stress, the by-product of a just and equitable society. It implies and demands a world freed from the poverty and servitude which often lead men to prefer war to the kind of peace they have to endure. It is, moreover, as much a means as an end; a method of peacefully regulating and changing the relations of states and peoples with each other.

Even so we can begin by defining peace as the absence of war. Negative though this definition is, it will serve well enough as a beginning since, as we have already suggested, there is little or no hope for the survival of civilised society in the era of nuclear weapons, unless at least large-scale war is abolished. It is true that justice and social progress for all men are a vital condition of a genuine peace. But it is no less true that until war has been abandoned as a method of achieving or seeking to achieve these ends, no adequate progress is possible and little justice either. The vicious circle of war and injustice can only be broken by actions at one and the same time to abolish war and to create the conditions of a true peace.

The forms of war

Here, however, the definition has to be taken a stage further. If the abandonment of war and the methods of war is a condition of peace, what does war mean in this context? For example: are war and violence the same thing? War is, without any doubt, the super-violence and all violence we can say, whether in the streets of Chicago or outside the Sorbonne in Paris or in London's Grosvenor Square or in front of the British Embassy in Peking, is a form of war. The rejection, or at least the control, of violence is as necessary to a peaceful and ordered domestic society as the rejection of war is to a peaceful and ordered world, and no sharp separation can be made between the two. But a study of violence in all its forms is outside the scope of this book. Our theme here is not violence in general but war in particular and war defined in the simplest terms as conflict between or within states fought usually but not always as we shall see, by military means.

War even in this definition can take a variety of forms. The two great wars of the present century are accurately described as world wars. They were fought over several continents and most if not all the oceans. They were fought between the most powerful states: Britain, France, Germany, Russia, the United States and Japan, with lesser allies on each side. Especially in the Second World War, thanks to aerial bombardment, the civilian populations of the states concerned were as much in the front line as the armed forces. By contrast the eighteen-day war over Kashmir in 1965 was limited to the two combatants, India and Pakistan, with no intervention by other states. The six-day war in the Middle East in June, 1967 was fought in the main by Israel and Egypt though with some active participation on the Egyptian side by other Arab states such as Syria and Jordan, and some moral support by the Soviet Union to Egypt and by the United States, France and Britain, to Israel. In Vietnam, the major combatants were the United States and South Vietnam on the one hand and North Vietnam and the South Vietnamese National Liberation Front (the Vietcong) on the other. But the Philippines, South Korea, Australia, and New Zealand sent contingents to fight with the Americans and the South Vietnamese, and the North Vietnamese received moral and material aid from the Russians and the Chinese. This we can say is war in its traditional form; the clash of arms between organised states which has punctuated history since nations began, and punctuated it so regularly that peace has often been thought of as simply the interval between wars.

Whether the present interval of peace between great wars which has lasted for twenty-five years can be prolonged indefinitely, is a question which we discuss later. It is possible that since global war fought with thermo-nuclear weapons (whose significance we discuss in Chapter Two) may well mean global destruction, the era of world wars may be coming to an end. But as the conflicts in Korea, the Middle East, Kashmir and Vietnam have shown, there are no signs that the flood of lesser wars is slackening. The table on the next page indicates that there have been twenty-eight lesser wars or outbreaks of hostilities (over 500 people killed) since 1945.

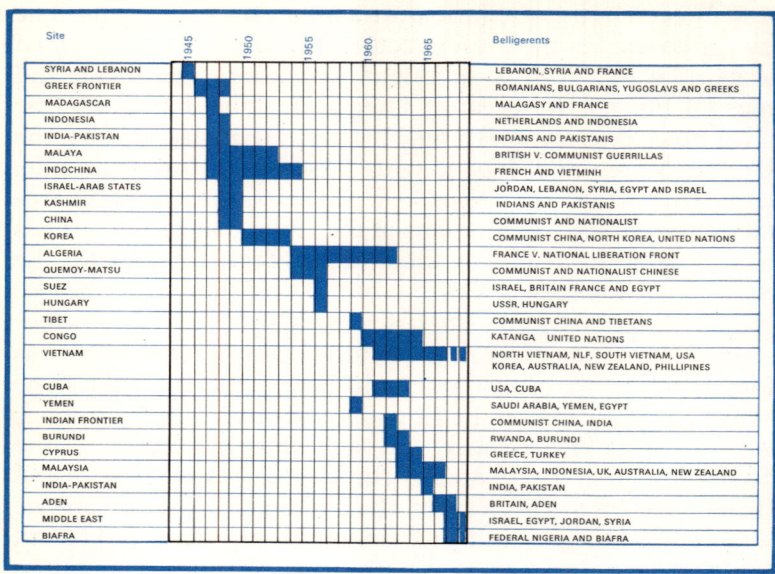

Site	1945	1950	1955	1960	1965	Belligerents
SYRIA AND LEBANON						LEBANON, SYRIA AND FRANCE
GREEK FRONTIER						ROMANIANS, BULGARIANS, YUGOSLAVS AND GREEKS
MADAGASCAR						MALAGASY AND FRANCE
INDONESIA						NETHERLANDS AND INDONESIA
INDIA-PAKISTAN						INDIANS AND PAKISTANIS
MALAYA						BRITISH V. COMMUNIST GUERRILLAS
INDOCHINA						FRENCH AND VIETMINH
ISRAEL-ARAB STATES						JORDAN, LEBANON, SYRIA, EGYPT AND ISRAEL
KASHMIR						INDIANS AND PAKISTANIS
CHINA						COMMUNIST AND NATIONALIST
KOREA						COMMUNIST CHINA, NORTH KOREA, UNITED NATIONS
ALGERIA						FRANCE V. NATIONAL LIBERATION FRONT
QUEMOY-MATSU						COMMUNIST AND NATIONALIST CHINESE
SUEZ						ISRAEL, BRITAIN FRANCE AND EGYPT
HUNGARY						USSR, HUNGARY
TIBET						COMMUNIST CHINA AND TIBETANS
CONGO						KATANGA UNITED NATIONS
VIETNAM						NORTH VIETNAM, NLF, SOUTH VIETNAM, USA KOREA, AUSTRALIA, NEW ZEALAND, PHILLIPINES
CUBA						USA, CUBA
YEMEN						SAUDI ARABIA, YEMEN, EGYPT
INDIAN FRONTIER						COMMUNIST CHINA, INDIA
BURUNDI						RWANDA, BURUNDI
CYPRUS						GREECE, TURKEY
MALAYSIA						MALAYSIA, INDONESIA, UK, AUSTRALIA, NEW ZEALAND
INDIA-PAKISTAN						INDIA, PAKISTAN
ADEN						BRITAIN, ADEN
MIDDLE EAST						ISRAEL, EGYPT, JORDAN, SYRIA
BIAFRA						FEDERAL NIGERIA AND BIAFRA

Hostilities since 1945

Nor are we likely to have seen the last of wars fought within the limits of the single state. Civil wars do not necessarily involve prolonged military conflict or military conflict on a large scale. There have been relatively bloodless but forcible seizures of power by one faction or party from another, or by the army from all other parties in, for example, many of the countries of Latin America including in recent times Brazil (1964), Argentine (1966) and Peru (1968). But the mid-nineteenth century war between eleven of the southern States of North America and the rest of the Union on the question of slavery, the bitter struggle between Republicans and Nationalists in the Spain of the 1930s and the recent war in mid-Africa between Federal Nigeria and the breakaway province of Biafra, have all shown that civil war can be as prolonged, and as destructive, as the war between separate states. In Nigeria, one hundred thousand Nigerians from one side or the other died in the first year of the fighting and at one

Traditional war :
left, Vietnam 1968,
interrogating a prisoner
below, London 1942, the
civilian takes it.

Civil war : Nigerians in conflict

period several thousand Biafrans, the indirect victims of the war, were dying daily of starvation and malnutrition.

Wars of liberation

To this catalogue of wars involving armed conflict, we must add another type of war not fought between independent states or factions within states but fought, often on uneven military terms, by subject peoples to free themselves from foreign domination. Insurrectional warfare has a long history and a mixed record of achievement. The American War of Independence of the later eighteenth century established the free United States of America. Sporadic war between British armed forces and the Irish Republican Army preceded the achievement of Irish independence in 1922. Resistance movements in German-occupied countries of the Second World War played a significant, and often heroic part, in bringing about the defeat of Hitler and his armed forces. The people of Hungary made an unsuccessful attempt in 1956 to gain more freedom for their country, only to find themselves overwhelmed by the military might of the Soviet Union. In southern Africa today, guerrilla forces mobilised and trained outside the area, wage a war of harassment and sabotage against the white governments of Rhodesia and of the Portuguese territories of Angola, Mozambique and Guinea, with at least the moral support of independent black African states to the north, and of sympathetic countries outside the African continent. Large areas of the Portuguese territories are under the control of the guerrillas despite the presence of considerable Portuguese armies. As the scale of this guerrilla fighting increases, so does the risk that these racial struggles will become the major source of war in the future and the spark that could set southern Africa ablaze.

The cold war

War in all these forms involves a clash of armed forces of differing severity and scale. But there is another type of war which can be fought without the firing of a single gun or the release of a single bomb. This is the type of war that Sun Tzu had in mind in 500 B.C. when he said that the supreme art of war was to subdue the enemy without fighting. From 1946 until the death of Stalin in 1953, the world situation was dominated by the 'cold war', as it was called, between the Soviet Union and its client communist states in Eastern Europe on the one side, and on the other the non-communist states of the West led by the United States. No shots were fired in this war but it was fought with the weapons of propaganda, subversion and misrepresentation as fiercely, though with no material destruction, as any war in history. We shall try to measure the significance of this type of conflict when we look at the relations today of the great powers of East and West. It is enough to say at this point, that if cold war is not war in the traditional sense, it is not peace either.

These then are the forms that war assumes or can assume in our time. First and most formidably, military conflict between single states or alliances of states fought with many, though not necessarily all the available weapons and involving increasingly all the peoples and all the resources of the states concerned. Second, the so-called civil wars, the internal struggles for power of factions or groups or regions within states, fought sometimes with the minimum of armed conflict but often in violent and prolonged encounters. Third, the revolutionary anti-colonial wars to overthrow alien or despotic governments resented by those they rule. And fourth and last, the cold war, or the war of nerves, waged by every mischief a country can inflict on another, short of military attack.

A true peace
It is in the light of these definitions of war that we have to return to our original question as to the nature and meaning of peace. The search for peace has to find its way through this maze of conflicts which darken and threaten to engulf the world. If peace has to put an end to all this, is it an attainable goal? How much peace can we sensibly expect to achieve given the aggressive impulses in the human spirit, given the force of competing nationalisms, given the unresolved political problems which separate the great nations, given the denial of vital freedoms to millions of people determined to gain them by fair means or foul? Is peace in these circumstances an idle dream, the vision merely of saints and seers, unable or unwilling to see the world as it is and to face its harsh realities? We return to this question in our final chapter. But we can say at once that peace is certainly an illusion if we think of it as a state of perpetual harmony in which no conflicts occur and from which all tensions have been magically dispelled. Tension is inseparable from all human relationships whether individual or collective. The problem is not to abolish the tensions, since that is impossible, but to ensure that they do not result in mutually destructive war. The problem in other words is not to abolish conflict, since that is out of the question, but to find the will and the way to resolve conflict by peaceful means and to create the international institutions that are required for this purpose. True peace then, is not a static condition at all but a dynamic process of growth and change which enriches spiritually and materially all the peoples of the world. We are, of course, caught up in this process already though we still have a long way to go. In the pages that follow we shall judge how far we have travelled towards the goal and what the prospects are of it being reached.

2

Weapons and peace

The war which is the clash of armed forces, clearly cannot be fought without weapons, but to abolish all weapons, assuming this to be practicable, is not to abolish all war automatically or to make certain that it cannot occur. Resort to war clearly becomes more difficult, if weapons are not readily available, or are available only in limited quantities, and this is one of the main reasons why armaments need to be reduced and controlled. But nations or groups bent on the preservation of their freedom or the defeat of aggressive attack, or on other ends which seem vital to them, will, if no peaceful solutions are readily to hand, provide themselves with the warlike weapons they need. Nor does the mere existence of weapons always and necessarily increase the risks of war, in the short term, as the possession of nuclear arms by the United States, the Soviet Union and Britain since 1950, has demonstrated. Even so an unchecked race in arms, now vastly increased in destructive power, creates a general insecurity, places heavy economic burdens on the countries involved in it and remains a grave threat to a peaceful world. A sizeable reduction of armaments, especially of the nuclear kind, by all or most of the nations possessing them, would make the world a safer place to live in and incidentally release substantial resources for peaceful purposes.

Recognising this, governments and statesmen have been trying continuously for nearly fifty years (except in the Second World War and the years immediately preceding it) to reach international agreements to stop the arms race and begin the process of reducing world armaments to safer levels. Their labours, as we shall see, have not been entirely fruitless but they are still a long way from their goal. There is still no general treaty limiting and controlling all types of armament, and there has been no solid reduction of armaments by international agreement since the Second World War ended.

By and large, the arms race goes on unchecked and the cost rises to astronomical proportions. In 1969, Britain was spending about £2,100 million a year on armaments, Germany a little less than this figure and France somewhat more. The United States spent about £22,000 million. The Soviet Union was estimated to have spent about £8,000 million and China about £3,000 million. We have to ask why so vital an enterprise fails to make progress and in what conditions it might succeed. But again we need to be clear first of all what it is we are talking about. What are we trying to abolish or reduce? What are armaments today and what are they likely to become in the world of the seventies?

Weapons today
It is customary to classify weapons under three major headings: conventional, nuclear or thermo-nuclear and chemical and biological. Conventional weapons are those traditional to the warfare of the present century—the rifles, guns and mortars of the land forces, the naval shells and torpedoes, and the bombs and rockets fired from aeroplanes. Nuclear weapons utilise the vastly increased explosive power generated by the controlled fission or fusion of atomic elements, packed into the warheads of missiles of varying range launched from land-based sites, carried by bombing 'planes, or delivered from submarines. Chemical and biological weapons, hitherto unused in large-scale warfare except to a limited degree in the First World War, utilise chemical substances or living organisms to kill or maim. (Chemicals were sprayed in Vietnam by low-flying American aircraft not to kill humans but to kill food plants and render the jungle unusable by the enemy.)

The application of nuclear power to the making of arms has opened up, as we shall see, an entirely new dimension of possible destruction in war. But it would be dangerously misleading to suggest that conventional armaments are weapons that inflict relatively little destruction. Both the world wars of the present century were fought with what would now be called conventional weapons, but in terms of losses in human life and the extent of material damage, they

*Conventional weapons : above, tank warfare in Flanders ;
below, the Grand Fleet sets sail.*

were immensely destructive in their effects. The scientific balance sheet of the mortality caused by the First World War gives the number of those who were killed or died of wounds as eight and a half million, with a further two million missing and presumed dead. Casualties in the Second World War have been calculated at a figure of sixteen million dead and twelve million wounded, with further casualties among civilians, mainly from aerial bombardment, of twenty million. One authoritative estimate cites the figure of one hundred million for the number of those who have died as the direct or indirect consequence of war in the two-thirds of the twentieth century that have now elapsed. Some of these were the casualties of the atom bombs dropped on Japan in the closing stages of the Second World War but most of them were victims of wars fought with conventional weapons—weapons whose destructive power has been increased four- or five-fold since 1945 alone.

The new dimension

All this, however, falls into relative insignificance when comparison is made with the potential destructiveness of the nuclear weapon which in its trial form marked the climax of the Second World War. The two experimental bombs dropped on the Japanese cities of Hiroshima and Nagasaki in August, 1945, killed or injured between them two hundred and twenty thousand people. In less than ten years after 1945, the development of the thermo-nuclear process, in which a fission reaction is used to start a fusion reaction and to increase substantially the amount of energy released, multiplied the power of nuclear weapons by another factor of a thousand and made possible the twenty-megaton hydrogen bomb having a destructive capacity, that is to say, of twenty million tons of explosive. The effects of the explosion of one bomb of this capacity at ground level on a city of a million inhabitants were set out thus in 1965 by a team of scientific experts for the Secretary-General of the United Nations:

killed by blast and fire: 270,000
killed by radio-active fall-out: 90,000
injured: 90,000

that is to say, a third of all the inhabitants would be killed as a result of blast or fire or from a radiation dose immediately received. All public services would be disrupted.

The same report estimated that a bomb of this calibre exploded over Manhattan would, in the absence of shelter or evacuation programmes, kill some six million of New York's eight million inhabitants and lead to an additional one million deaths beyond the city limits. Writing as long ago as 1960, two American scientists, Harrison Brown and James Neal made a comparison showing that if the explosive power (1,000 tons) of the biggest bomb used in the Second World War is represented by a one-foot ruler standing on its end, the atom bombs dropped over Japan in 1945 would be represented by the height of the Empire State Building in New York (1,472 feet), and the twenty-megaton (20 million tons) hydrogen bomb of today by the height of the orbit of the Soviet Sputnik 1. Since this comparison was made, there have been ten further years of progress in bomb-making.

Fracturing the future

Inevitably in the early stages, there was some exaggeration of the destructive possibilities of this new form of warfare. Even the use of the more advanced thermo-nuclear weapon of today would not cause the world to disappear in a ball of fire, as the early commentators suggested. But it is beyond argument that the modern ballistic missile, armed with a thermo-nuclear warhead or possibly several separate warheads, releases a force far more destructive than anything yet known in human experience. Wayland Young writing nearly twenty years ago on the indirect effects of a moderate-sized nuclear bomb dropped on London, said that 'for a hundred miles or so downwind, the land would be poisoned for years, the vegetation would change from an overall green to an overall grey with morbid growths—and there is no defence against it.' It is this power to inflict damage, not only immediately but on the earth and its peoples for generations to come, that underlines the distinction between the conventional and the thermo-nuclear weapon of today. 'The uniqueness of our time in history', said Norman Cousins, a leading American editor, '. . . is that we are now able to fracture and fragment the

human future on earth . . . we can pulverise human civilisation; we can upset the vital balances in atmosphere, in soil and
in water that sustain life. In brief, we can deprive man of
his future.'

Gases and germs

Though the thermo-nuclear bomb is a weapon of dreadful
and dreaded power, it is not the only mass-destruction weapon
available for use in war. Much is heard of nuclear weapons
because the world has seen them in use over Japan and
because the test explosions they require, can hardly be concealed even if they take place underground. Preparations for
chemical and biological warfare on the other hand, can be
fully concealed unless public pressure obliges governments to
reveal them. They are carried out in closely-guarded establish-
ments such as Fort Detrick in the United States, Suffield in
Canada, Porton Down in Britain and their unnamed counter-
parts in the Soviet Union and elsewhere. Here are produced or
examined, inert chemical substances such as gas sprays and
defoliants which kill by poisoning, and biological weapons
consisting of living organisms that cause progressive disease
in men, animals and plants. 'These are weapons', said Michael
Pearson, 'both bizarre and terrifying; gases that cannot be
detected but kill in minutes, that paralyse or hallucinate or
depress to the point of cowardice, or that merely cause
vomiting or choking or weeping; germs that can cause a wide
range of diseases in men and animals, chemicals that can
wither food crops or defoliate jungles.' Moreover, the techniques of chemical and biological weapon-making are
relatively inexpensive and so within the means of almost every
country. An added difficulty of control is that even more
potent compounds, which could be used for warlike purposes,
are being discovered daily in the constant search for more
effective medicinal drugs.

Nuclear and biological weapons are available for use now
but even more unconventional weapons are being dreamed
up by the scientists. 'Simulated Acts of God already labelled
for tomorrow's armoury' said the Science Correspondent of
The Guardian include 'guided hurricanes, disastrous tidal

Above, on the way to nuclear weapons—the German V.2 of 1944: opposite, a nuclear weapon, the Polaris missile, lifts off.

waves and sudden holes in the protective ozone layer of the Earth which allow high energy radiated from the sun to burn selected areas to death.'

No effective defence
Against mass-destruction weapons of this character there is no effective defence, if by effective we mean the power to destroy the enemy's offensive weapon and prevent it reaching its target. The only defence (and it defends only if it *does* deter the enemy from using his weapon) is the power to inflict as great or greater damage on the enemy by retaliation. There are no known antidotes to chemical and biological weapons, though it can be assumed that scientists in laboratories throughout the world are trying to discover them. The United States was said to be spending in 1964 about £100 million a year on this form of research alone, and a leading British specialist in chemical and biological warfare has claimed that between fifteen and twenty per cent of Soviet Russia's munition stockpile, including rockets and missiles, is filled with chemical weapons. Research into these weapons is often claimed, in Britain for example, to be justified on the ground that it is directed solely to this defensive purpose.

As for nuclear weapons, it is beyond dispute that a holocaust will befall, not only the countries involved but their near-neighbours also, once strategic nuclear warfare begins. In theory, it is possible to intercept and destroy ballistic missiles fired at continental range, but only one missile has to get through to create massive destruction. The Russians have built an anti-missile system intended to deflect and destroy any American missile directed at Moscow and its surroundings. The United States has committed itself, subject to possible disarmament agreements, to the provision of a similar anti-missile system, intended to protect American cities, or at least its own missile launching sites, from attack. But there can be no certainty that the anti-missile will counter the missile. The operation has been described as trying to hit a tennis ball in the air with another tennis ball, and the only likely development of anti-missile missile systems would be a more dangerous speeding-up of the arms race.

Even so, we have to recognise that equality or near-equality in armaments between two countries or two groups of allies, can act as a restraining influence and serve to maintain peace, if only for a time. The historic theory of the balance of power is based on the assumption that, given broadly equal military strengths between nations or groups of nations, there is little likelihood of war between them. War only becomes probable or certain, according to this theory, when the balance is upset and the military advantage tipped decisively in favour of one side or the other. The principle can be said to have operated in the field of nuclear weapons during the twenty-year period when these weapons were the virtual monopoly of the United States and the Soviet Union. The certainty, that a nuclear attack by one party or the other would bring instant and effective retaliation, had a sobering influence on the behaviour of both countries and obliged them to handle their relations with each other in such a way as to avoid the mutual and mortal peril of involvement in nuclear war. 'If Cain can only murder brother Abel by murdering himself, who then can claim the birthright?'

This balance of power, or balance of terror, might have had a steadying influence indefinitely, if the Soviet Union and the United States had been able to keep their virtual monopoly of nuclear weapons. The monopoly has now been broken, however, by other countries; some, like France and China, are already on the threshold of possessing nuclear weapons and the means of delivering them, others are rapidly nearing the position where the production of these weapons is at least technically possible. Writing in 1966, Lord Chalfont, then Britain's chief negotiator in disarmament discussions, suggested that even if the nuclear stalemate had existed and to a degree acted beneficially, it was nevertheless arguable that the balance no longer existed. And even if it did still mean something, it was likely, he argued, that the political and economic pressures of the next ten to fifteen years would destroy it completely. In fact, he concluded, there seemed no reason why China, if she so wished, should not in an even shorter period decisively upset this precarious balance and 'destroy the last illusions of the nuclear stalemate.'

The Chinese Bomb

Perhaps no exceptional insight was needed to make this prophecy; the signs could be read by all who chose to read them. China exploded her first nuclear device in October, 1964. Since then she has conducted at least seven nuclear weapon tests. In the early 1970s, she can be expected to be able to deliver a thermo-nuclear warhead in the inter-continental ballistic missile class, with a yield of explosive in the megaton range (twenty million tons of explosive). Lord Chalfont was rightly able to conclude that the world was moving 'into a period of unprecedented dangers in the international balances of power.'

The fear of retaliation would continue to discourage the use of nuclear weapons and other weapons of mass-destruc-tion, even if the membership of the nuclear weapon club were to increase. But the spread of nuclear weapons to yet more countries adds to the uncertainty which the existence of these weapons creates, and complicates the problem of achieving a general and controlled disarmament, while making the task more urgent and essential. It adds also to another danger implicit in the nuclear arms race—the possibility that the weapons may be used accidentally by a country in the mistaken assumption that they are about to be used against it. 'You may require' said Wayland Young (Lord Kennet) speaking of safeguards against accidental use, 'precise actions by twenty men before a nuclear bomb or rocket is fired and reduce the chance of error to x over a function of twenty. You may select level-headed men and train them in their awful responsibility, and you may build-in mechanical and electronic barriers against mistakes in a 'fail-safe' system, but you can never do more than reduce and still further reduce the chances of error. You cannot make error impossible.'

The quest for disarmament

These are the dangers which in the present century have prompted the League of Nations, the United Nations and succeeding generations of statesmen, to try and bring the arms race under control and reduce the burden of war preparations on all the nations. Their efforts began in the modern phase

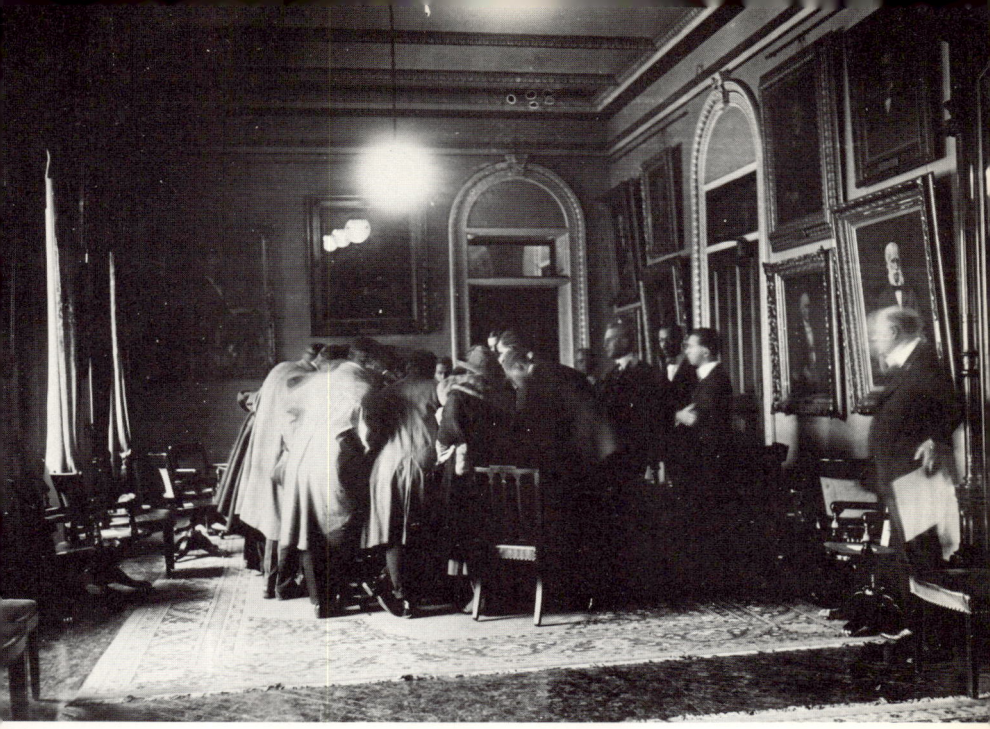

Journalists look at the Washington Naval Treaty on the day of signing.

with the close of the First World War. The Treaty of Versailles which brought that war to a formal end, and made the peace at the dictation of the victorious Allied powers, imposed on a defeated Germany drastic measures of disarmament intended to make it impossible for her to resume her policy of military aggression. The treaty forbade her to possess battleships, aircraft carriers and submarines; it denied her a conscript army, tanks, poison gas and other weapons; it limited her army to 100,000 men and forbade her a military airforce.

The intention was that this enforced disarmament of Germany and her former allies should be extended later to all countries. But since preparation for a general treaty was bound to take time and a dangerous race in naval armaments was already beginning, the United States, Britain and Japan, as the leading naval powers, made the Washington Naval Treaty of 1922 which reduced by 40% the existing strengths of the three navies in certain types of warship and instituted 'a naval holiday' under which no new battleships were to be built for ten years. The treaty led to a lessening of tension between Japan and America and eight years later its provisions were extended, in a London Conference, to cover other classes of naval vessels not limited in 1922. These treaties were relatively short-lived but they brought about the only major reduction and limitation of weapons, achieved by international treaty, in the fifty years that have elapsed since the end of the First World War.

The World Disarmament Conference

Meanwhile, preliminary talks under the League of Nations, aimed at a general disarmament treaty, had been taking place in commissions and technical committees, from the start of the League in 1919. The preparation was to culminate in the World Disarmament Conference, the first and to-date the last of its kind, which opened in Geneva in February, 1932 under the chairmanship of a British statesman, Arthur Henderson. Widespread public support for the Conference had been expressed throughout the world. The technical problems of reducing armaments had been exhaustively considered and hopes were high that the partial successes of the Washington and London treaties would be repeated on a universal basis, and over the whole range of weapons. Unfortunately, the political work of the governments lagged behind the work of the experts and a year was to elapse before, for instance, the British Government laid before the Conference a comprehensive draft disarmament convention which the then British Foreign Secretary, Anthony Eden, had prepared. More seriously than this, the Conference was to be caught up in the hostile winds of world events. Hitler had come to power in Germany in 1933 and had begun to rearm Germany in defiance of the Treaty of Versailles. The fears already created by Japan's seizure of Manchuria, which occurred before the Conference opened, were sharply increased by the rapid growth of German Nazism and Italian Fascism. In such a climate, the success of the Conference became virtually impossible and early in 1934, it came to a fruitless and inglorious end. Rearmament, rather than disarmament, became the order of the day.

Disarming the defeated

In six years of war from 1939 to 1945, world armaments inevitably reached unprecedented levels. The peace, when it came in 1945, almost stripped the defeated Germans and Japanese of their navies and armies, denied them military air forces and forbade them to introduce compulsory military service. Britain's army of 5 million in 1945 was reduced in four years to 770,000; the United States reduced its armed forces from 12 million in 1945 to 1·5 million in 1947. This was a substantial reduction in armaments from the peak levels of 1945. But, even in Britain and the United States, the armed forces that remained were respectively nearly twice and three times the size of those they possessed in 1939. In the case of the Soviet Union, there were not even comparable reductions after 1945; Russia kept 5 to 6 million men in her armies and began the naval building which was to make her, in time, one of the major sea powers. Moreover the era of mass-destruction weapons, in a truly literal sense, had begun with the explosion of the first atomic bombs. It became even more necessary to lessen the economic burdens of armaments and to reduce the dangers of the arms race. Not surprisingly, the United Nations, taking up the cause laid down by the defunct League, set general and controlled disarmament among its major objectives and the latest chapters of the disarmament story began.

The United Nations steps in

By its first resolution, the first General Assembly of the United Nations, meeting in January 1946, acknowledged the challenge posed by nuclear weapons and set up an Atomic Energy Commission. One of its main tasks was to be the preparation of proposals for the abolition of atomic armaments and all other weapons of mass destruction, and for the setting-up of a system of international inspection to ensure that the treaty would be carried out. A year later the Security Council acting on the basis of a unanimous resolution of the General Assembly of December 1946, set up a Commission for Conventional Armaments to prepare plans for the reduction of non-nuclear weapons and armed forces. For fifteen years, the

United Nations tried to carry out the two-fold purpose of these original bodies. From March, 1962 onwards, the discussions were centred in the Eighteen-nation Disarmament Conference (some additional nations were brought in, in 1969) meeting in Geneva and made up of five countries from the North Atlantic Treaty Organisation (NATO), five from the 'Eastern' communist countries (members of the Warsaw Pact) and some neutral or 'non-aligned' countries assumed to be politically independent and not tied to one or other of the big powers.

It would be easy to take a cynical view of all these proceedings and say that the nations have done everything about disarmament, except disarm. It is unfortunately true, as we have already noted, that despite nearly fifty years of effort no general disarmament by international agreement has taken place. But the twenty-five years of negotiation under the United Nations have not been entirely without result. Agreement has been reached on the principles of disarmament, and to some extent on ways and means of carrying it out, once an adequate will to disarm exists. Beyond that, some steps have been taken in the last ten years which, while involving no actual reduction or abolition of armaments, have helped to lessen world tensions, to limit in some degree the dangers of the arms race and to prepare the ground for some tangible disarmament in the future. In 1963, the so-called 'hot-line'— the special direct telegraph and teleprinter link between Soviet and American statesmen for use in times of crisis and danger of war, was opened between Washington and Moscow. (In 1967, a similar link was created between Moscow and London). In 1963, a treaty was made banning the testing of nuclear weapons in the atmosphere and under the sea, though not under the ground—an agreement which, though it did not stop testing by the Chinese and the French, did sensibly reduce the amount of atomic radiation injected into the atmosphere. In the same year the Soviet Union and the United States agreed not to put nuclear weapons into orbit in outer space.

Five years later came the first agreements designed to prevent the emergence of new nuclear-weapon powers, if not

Britain, Russia, America sign the
Non-Proliferation Treaty, London, July, 1968.

to reduce or abolish the nuclear weapons already in existence. In January 1968, after long discussion, the United States and the Soviet Union jointly tabled draft proposals for an international Non-proliferation Treaty designed to prevent the spread of nuclear weapons to nations not already possessing them, at least six of whom—West Germany, India, Canada, Italy, Poland and Sweden—were believed, even at that time, to have the resources enabling them to afford and achieve a small nuclear capability. In June 1968, the Soviet-American draft treaty was adopted almost unanimously by the United Nations and made open for the signature of any nations ready to accept it. On 21st July it was signed simultaneously in Washington, Moscow and London, by the United States, the Soviet Union and Britain and at the same time, by sixty smaller, non-nuclear countries. The treaty came into force in March 1970 when the necessary number of States had deposited instruments of ratification.

Two significant events accompanied the signing of this Non-proliferation Treaty. The United States and the

Soviet Union coupled with their sponsorship of the treaty, an undertaking, to which Britain is also a party, to come to the aid of any country not possessing nuclear weapons, which is the victim of, or is threatened by, nuclear attack. The assumption was that such an assurance would encourage the non-nuclear countries to forego the possession of their own nuclear weapons. The significance of this was that the world's two super-powers were giving together, for the first time, direct guarantees of protection for smaller countries—a pledge which might become in the long run the basis of an effective and general system of protective guarantees for smaller nations under the United Nations. Beyond this, the two super-powers announced on the day they signed to Non-proliferation Treaty that they intended to enter into fresh discussions aimed at the limitation of their nuclear weapon systems, and especially the prevention of an extended race in the production of anti-ballistic missile screens. At the same time the Soviet Union sent to all governments a memorandum calling for talks in Geneva on a nine-point disarmament pro-gramme (not all the points were new) ranging from a ban on the production and use of nuclear weapons to an agreement to ensure the peaceful use of the ocean floor.

The objectors
How far the Non-proliferation Treaty will succeed in its object of preventing the spread of nuclear weapons to countries at present non-nuclear, remains to be seen. China took a hostile view of the negotiations and has not signed it. France also refused to sign, though she undertook to regard herself as bound by its main provisions. Several countries among those already mentioned as having a near-nuclear capacity, for example West Germany, India and Italy, also re-fused to sign the treaty at the outset because they feared that it would limit their freedom to use nuclear processes for peaceful uses, or because they objected to the fact that the sponsors of the treaty were not at the same time reducing or limiting their own nuclear weapons. In some cases these objections were strengthened by fears and uncertainties created by the Soviet invasion of Czechoslovakia in August, 1968.

The success of the treaty in its direct purpose remained uncertain, but its adoption encouraged the Geneva Disarmament Conference to press on to further objectives including the extension of the agreement banning certain nuclear weapon tests to cover all testing of nuclear arms, an attempt to check the uncontrolled production and distribution of plutonium, which is the raw material from which nuclear weapons are made, and to bring the dangers of chemical and biological warfare under effective control. In 1969, Britain proposed to the Geneva Conference the adoption of a convention banning biological weapons and early in 1970 the President of the United States announced American intentions to call a halt to preparations for chemical and biological warfare.

The shadow of China

As for the two super-powers, the importance of their joint sponsorship of the Non-proliferation Treaty, and of their decision to continue talking, was that it showed that they are able to cooperate in fields of disarmament in which they have a common interest. The sheer necessity for both of them to avoid, if possible, the immense costs of an anti-missile missile race may compel them to call this race off before it has got fully into its stride. Whether they can go beyond that point to a real beginning of the reduction of their nuclear weapons, will depend on a number of mainly political factors, the chief of which are the lack of confidence created by such happenings as the Soviet invasion of Czechoslovakia and, in the minds of both the United States and the Soviet Union, uncertainty as to the role of China as a nuclear power. No radical reduction of nuclear weapons, or any other armaments, by the United States and the Soviet Union is likely, unless China can be brought within the scope of the agreement, and this in turn may depend not only on events within China itself but also on the ability of the world outside China to bring her out of her isolation, into the society of nations at the United Nations and elsewhere. The smaller countries may be able to do something to keep the disarmament issue alive and to spur the great powers on to a fulfilment of their disarmament pledges, but it is only great-power agreement that can truly resolve the disarmament problem. In 1964, Lord Ritchie-Calder calculated that in their nuclear stockpiles alone, the great powers had the equivalent of 320,000 million tons of explosive, representing 100 tons of destructive power for every man, woman and child on earth. The bulk of the armaments in the world are theirs and most of the disarmament must come from them.

Why the delay?

One final and more fundamental question presents itself in this matter of armaments and disarmament. Why, despite the benefits that would result from a general and radical reduction in world armaments, does it prove so difficult to reach even limited agreements on disarmament and take so long to negotiate them? Perhaps we get a clue to the answer, if we recognise that armaments are as much a symptom, or a sign, of insecurity as a cause. They contribute to insecurity over-all, but they are not its sole or primary cause. Great powers insist on maintaining their armaments, basically because they mistrust the intentions of other great powers and also because, though they may be reluctant to acknowledge it, they fear the threat to their security and their power, of the revolutionary movements or the counter-revolutionary movements that sweep the world. The smaller countries insist on having a military capacity of their own, either because they too, distrust their neighbours or because there is, as yet, no adequate international system to guarantee their security and their legitimate national aspirations. Unfree and under-privileged peoples seek arms or resort to arms, because too often they are led to feel that only the possession and the use of arms will gain them political freedom and the economic place in the sun they deserve and demand. Reliance on armaments and violence may well prove disastrous for all concerned in the longer run and in the meantime they absorb, as we have said, resources which could be better used. It is vital that the effort to reduce them by international agreement should continue unceasingly. But until there is more conviction among states and peoples that the reasonable ends they seek, can be gained by peaceful means, and especially by the development of a world system of peace under law through the United Nations, it seems unlikely that they will be persuaded to lay aside their arms or renounce the right to resort, if need be, to the ultimate sanction of war and violence. General and radical disarmament, in other words, will become more feasible as the peace-keeping powers of the United Nations are strengthened and when at least some progress has been made in resolving the great issues which divide and disturb the world. It is to these decisive issues that we now turn.

TOPICS FOR DISCUSSION

- Would you say that the development of nuclear armaments and other mass-destruction weapons, has increased or lessened the probability of war?

- Why is it that, despite the dangers of the arms race and all the efforts that have been made to negotiate a disarmament treaty, so little real disarmament has been achieved?

- What are the arguments for Great Britain 'going it alone' in reducing its armaments, whatever other nations may do or not do?

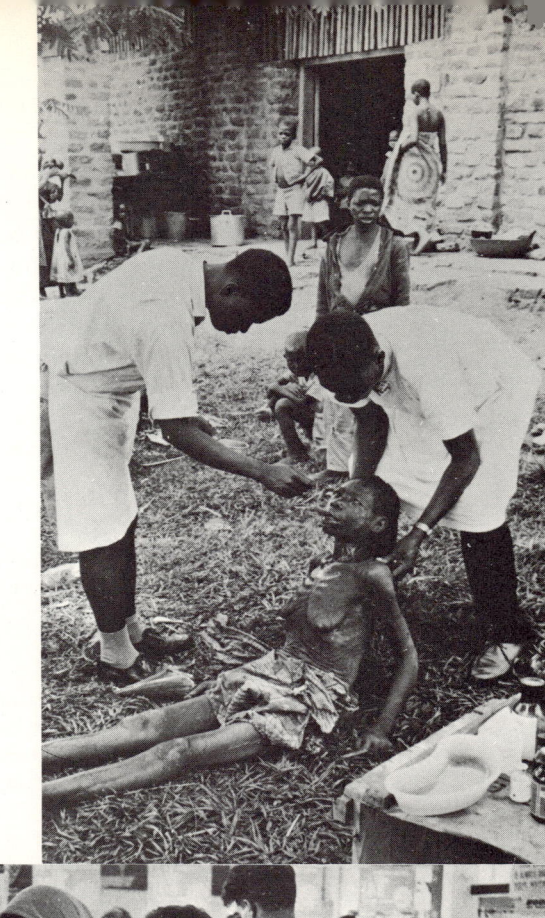

Rich world—poor world:
opposite, famine in the
Congo; below, the
affluent West

3

Rich world, poor world

We could say that there are at the international level three major sources of tension and of conflict, actual or potential, in the world today. First the problem of world poverty—the gap between the wealth and living standards of the prosperous countries of the northern hemisphere, for the most part, and the impoverished and under-developed countries, lying mainly on or near the Equator in Asia, Africa and Latin America. Related, if only geographically, to this crisis of poverty and wealth, is the conflict of race and colour, centred largely in Africa but finding its sympathetic echoes in other parts of the world. And thirdly, there is the East-West problem—the political and ideological rivalry of the communist and non-communist great powers and their associates, now changing in character under the influence of the divisions that have developed within both East and West.

We speak hopefully of one world, but in terms of riches and poverty and of comparative standards of living, there are two worlds. Fifteen per cent of the people of the world who live in North America, Western Europe, the Soviet Union and in other areas of relative prosperity, own between them some 90% of the world's wealth, defined in terms of capital resources and national income. Their countries produce half the world's wheat, 70% of all meat and, significantly in terms of food values, 80% of the world's protein. They possess an even larger percentage of the world's gold reserves. The average annual income per person (that is the total national income divided by the total population) in these richer, industrialised countries amounts to £700 a year and even if the United States, where the average national income rises to £1,300 a year, is omitted, the average income for the 340 million people of Western Europe is about £350 a year.

Several of these rich countries have their own 'pockets' of poverty—there are said to be, for example, ten to fourteen

million hungry Americans in the South and South-West—
but the overall picture is one of general affluence and comfort.

The under-privileged
The other world is the world of the poor and the under-
privileged; the three-quarters or more of mankind who live
for the most part at or below the subsistence level. This is the
world of Africa, excluding southern Africa; of the Americas,
excluding Canada and the United States; of Asia, including
the Middle East, and of scattered areas in Western and Eastern
Europe including Greece. About 80 of the 126 member states
of the United Nations are classified as developing countries,
the term they themselves prefer to backward or under-
developed. These states contain four-fifths of the world's 3·3
thousand million people. Their average annual income is less
than £45 a year, one fifteenth of the average in the rich world.
In India, to take a single though extreme example, 520 million
people have an average annual income of less than £25 a year.
Out of the total Indian population, less than 1% have an
annual income per head equal to the average income of the
citizens of the United States. The sum the United States
spends on defence alone, is 60% greater than the entire
national income of India, though India has two and a half
times the population of the United States.

These are mere figures. They convey little, in themselves, of
the grim realities of want and hardship which underlie
differences of income and comparisons set out in money
terms. Poverty, in any case, is not an isolated feature; it goes
hand in hand with social conditions which are typical of all
or most of the developing countries—a high rate of increase
in population; an abnormal prevalence of disease and under-
nourishment; exceptional dependence on the uncertain
production of a single crop or a single mineral; and a high rate
of unemployment or underemployment. It is vividly illustrated by infant mortality rates which range from 12·6 infant
deaths per 1,000 live births in a developed country such as
Sweden to 150 or more per 1,000 in some developing
countries. In India, 48% of all the children die before they are

five years old. Many children in developing areas, live beyond
the age of one year but fail to reach the age of five years. Many
more die before they become adult.

High death rates reflect the natural hazards under which
many millions of people in these areas have to live; but they
also reflect inadequate health services and conditions of
chronic under-feeding and near-starvation. Two out of every
three persons in the world are under-nourished; every other
person is abnormally prone to disease because his diet lacks
the essential vitamins, proteins and minerals. Every day in
every year, 8,000–10,000 people die because they are underfed
and lack resistance to disease. Moreover, these deficiencies are
aggravated for more than a thousand million people, by the
housing conditions in which they have to live. Most of the
towns in the developing countries have their densely-
overcrowded shanty areas, many of which lack sewers, water
or roads. Even in country areas the shacks of the rural workers,
as a United Nations report once put it, 'are only a little less
miserable because of their larger rations of light and air.'

The widening gap
These are the facts of life in two-thirds of the world today.
This is the present gulf between the resources and the living
conditions of the peoples of the rich world and the poor world.
The situation might be tolerable, if the gap was being steadily
narrowed; in fact it grows wider every day. It is true that the
poor are getting marginally less poor but at a rate far slower
than the rate at which the rich become richer. The misery of
the developing world deepens, and for reasons which are not
hard to find. It is here, as the graph on the next page shows,
that population grows at the fastest rate. The poor world has a
net annual increase in population of about 2·5%. The richer
nations have an average increase of only 1·1%. More than
50,000 babies are born daily in India; 30,000 daily in China.
By the year 2006, the world's population will have doubled;
but most of these people will live in the poorer areas unless, in
the meantime, energetic steps have been taken to limit
populations in the countries concerned. By the end of this
century the percentage increase of population over today's

figure will be 29% in Europe; in the United States it will be 78%; in Asia 100%; in Africa 181%; in Latin America not far short of 200%. The poor could then number, it has been estimated, four-fifths of all the people in the world.

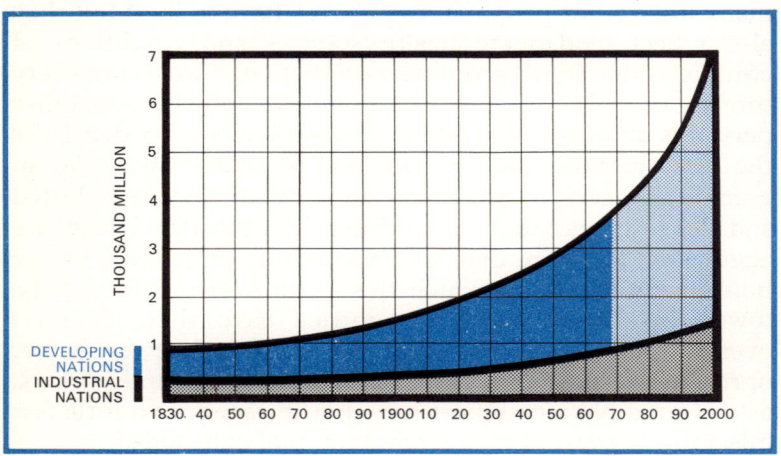

Growth in world population from 1830 to 2000

But even if their populations grow faster, will not the poorer countries become relatively better off in economic terms than they are today? The answer in over-all terms must be 'No'. The developing countries are at present increasing their gross national product—which is the value of all the goods and services they have available in a given year for use or investment—by about 4·8%, or 2·3% per head. The advanced countries of the North and West are increasing their gross national product at an annual average of 5%, or 3·9% per head. At the present rate of increase in the poor countries, the £40 to £50 of annual income per head, compounded for thirty years will become about £90 in the year 2000. At an annual rate of growth increase of 3·9% per head, the present annual income per head of the rich countries (which is £700), compounded for thirty years, becomes £2,000 by the end of the century. The gap between the average annual incomes per head of the rich and the poor nations will then be three times as big as it is today.

The passionate demand

What has all this to do with the problems of war and peace? Professor Gunnar Myrdal, the Swedish economist, has described the connection between poverty and war as, 'no more than a popular theory . . . unrelated in any way to reality'. Most wars, he argues, do not stem from poverty but from other causes. If war is defined in traditional terms, or visualised in global terms, this may be true. Only the relatively advanced nations have the technical knowledge or the industrial capacity for the waging of large-scale modern war. The threat to peace in this sense, does not come from the poorer nations. But if massive poverty is not a provocation to aggressive war, it is an incitement to violence and revolt, especially now that the deprived peoples are learning of the better world that might be theirs. In what has been called 'the revolution of rising expectations', two-thirds of the world's people are no longer content to accept poverty, disease and near-starvation as the ordained fate of themselves and their children. They insist on a greater and fairer share of the riches and resources of the common world. 'The distant dream', as Paul G. Hoffman of the United Nations has put it, 'has become the passionate demand.'

The background of aid

We do not know yet whether the nations, and especially the richer ones, will respond in time to the challenge of this situation and enable the poverty crisis to be overcome by peaceful means. The signs are not too encouraging. But strenuous, if still inadequate efforts have already been made over the last quarter of a century, to promote the development of the poor world and to improve the living conditions of its peoples. The greater part of this assistance has been provided on a bilateral basis through transactions between two individual countries, one giving or lending aid, the other receiving it. The rest has been channelled to the receiving countries on an international basis, through the operations of the United Nations and its Specialised Agencies, to which we later refer.

Between 1950, when large-scale assistance to the developing countries began, and 1962, the volume of aid distributed

1966	Gross official aid in United States dollars	Percentage of National Income
Australia	129 m.	0·67
Austria	37 m.	0·49
Belgium	92 m.	0·64
Canada	208 m.	0·52
Denmark	26 m.	0·30
France	721 m.	0·95
Germany	490 m.	0·54
Italy	117 m.	0·24
Japan	285 m.	0·37
Netherlands	95 m.	0·55
Norway	13 m.	0·23
Portugal	24 m.	0·70
Sweden	56 m.	0·34
United Kingdom	501 m.	0·60
United States of America	3,634 m.	0·60
Total	6,432 m.	Average 0·57

The major donors

increased in a steady progression by about 12%. Since 1962, the trend has been changed and aid to the poor world from the rich world has levelled off so that in 1966 it was only 8% higher than in 1962.

The total amounts of aid provided in 1966 by the major donor countries under bilateral arrangements (that is arrangements made directly between the giver and the receiver) and multilaterally through international agencies, are shown in the table above.

In 1966, total assistance to the developing countries amounted to about 6,432 million dollars (gross) a year, or approximately £2,000 million—a figure which, though it appears large, represented only one thirty-fifth of the total world armaments bill of the same year and about the amount Britain alone was spending on military defence. The United States, as the largest and richest donor, contributed over half of the total aid, devoting on political grounds the greater part of its assistance to countries close to, and possibly threatened by, the chief communist powers and liable, because of their economic conditions, to fall prey to Communism. The Soviet

Union contributed about a thirteenth of the assistance given by the United States and, again with political and strategic considerations in mind, sent its aid to countries where, hopefully, Soviet Communist influence might be increased. The group of 'middle' countries giving aid—Britain, France, Belgium, Portugal and Holland—have tended to channel their assistance towards their ex-colonies in Asia and Africa, though latterly Britain has included countries outside the Commonwealth altogether. By 1966 the donor countries also included West Germany and Japan, earlier absorbed in their own post-war reconstruction, Canada, Australia and the countries of Scandinavia.

Donors and receivers
The richer the country, the easier it is, of course, for it to finance its aid programme and the aid the same countries gave in 1966 is also set out as a percentage of their national income in the table. It will be seen that none of the countries listed were giving in 1966 the 1% of their national income they had pledged themselves to provide. The United States gives most but comes equal fifth in the list of percentages and indeed two years later, in 1968, according to the World Bank's Pearson Report on Development Aid, the U.S.A. ranked seventh in the percentage of G.N.P. devoted to official aid. Britain's official economic aid to the developing countries has increased by about two and a half times since 1956 and together with private aid now represents some four-fifths of one per cent of the country's gross national product. In 1969, total British government aid, including bilateral grants and loans and the contribution through international agencies, amounted to £215 million. The average annual aid given by the Soviet Union is about £100 million.

As the resources of the donor countries vary, so do the needs of the receiving countries, according, in the main, to the size of their populations. India gets more absolute aid than any other single country but she has a population now of more than 500 million, and in relative terms she receives therefore comparatively little. Asia as a whole, though among the most needy areas of the world, received, in fact, least help in proportion to population, the rate being in 1966, £1 3s 8d per person. The countries of South and Central America received £1 10s 0d per head; the figure for Africa was £2 5s 0d.

The forms of aid

Aid is given in money or in technical assistance or sometimes in kind, the 'kind' including relief supplies in emergency situations. All the poorer countries need capital for the building of roads, factories, railways and other essential projects. When funds are not provided in the form of grants—and these account for about half the total monetary aid given—the receiving countries are lent money at low rates of interest and on a long-term repayment plan. They now tend to pay even less for the money they borrow but, nevertheless, too much of the wealth created by development, is used up simply in the payment of interest and the repayment of the debt itself. Figures given by the Administrator of the United Nations Development Programme in June 1968, showed that while 6,000 million dollars of financial aid from outside went in 1966 into the developing countries in the form of capital investment, more than half this sum—3·9 thousand million dollars—was absorbed in the same year in interest on, and the repayment of, foreign loans. Beyond this official monetary aid, is the investment of privately-owned capital in the developing countries and this represents, in fact, a substantial proportion of the total aid provided. In form, it is like any other monetary aid and can be put to the same kind of purpose as aid through governments. But it is looked on less favourably by the receiving governments, who fear that private business under the influence of the profit motive, will not reinvest enough of its surplus profits in the receiving country and so fail to increase the national wealth.

The poor world cannot do without this financial assistance from outside in the period of capital development. But the developing countries actually finance 80% of their capital investment themselves by tightening their belts and depriving themselves for the time-being of consumer benefits which they might otherwise provide for their peoples. Four-fifths of the

A young volunteer teaches art in Jamaica

resources needed for development have to come, in other words, from domestic savings. India, for example, needs an investment of £1,250 million a year for her fourth Five-Year Development Plan but she receives only a quarter of this from the outside world. The Indian people, who live on an average £00·06 a day, have to provide the rest of the money required at the cost of postponing desperately-needed immediate improvements in their standard of living. Their numbers are increasing moreover at a net figure of thirteen millions a year. An Indian baby is born every second and a half.

Person-to-person assistance to the poor world is given both directly and through international agencies, by the veritable army of technicians drawn from the developed countries who contribute their skills in a variety of ways, from research into soil erosion to the designing and equipping of hospitals, schools, factories and other public works. In 1967, some 10,000 people recruited by the British Government alone were engaged in technical assistance work overseas. In addition, large numbers of publicly-financed teachers, doctors, and other professional people work for longer or shorter periods in the developing countries. Beyond these still, are the short-term and mostly young volunteers who work on unskilled tasks wherever the need is, and come mainly from North America and Western Europe, under such schemes as the Peace Corps of the United States and Voluntary Service Overseas in Britain.

Because of the differing political interests and the special relations of particular donor countries to particular receiving countries, the 90% of aid given bilaterally since 1950, has been spread widely, though much too thinly, over the areas of greatest need. But there is inevitably some overlapping in the giving or the lending (not always, admittedly, a bad thing for the receiving country) and, as we have already noted, assistance given directly by single countries is always liable to have political strings attached to it and to be coloured by the national self-interest of the donor. Hence the importance of multilateral aid, which is aid channelled through the United Nations and its various agencies. Though this amounts to only 9% of the total aid given, it does bring an impartial international element into the transaction between giver and receiver and represents a vital factor in the whole process of aid and development.

The rôle of the United Nations

From the beginning, the declared purposes of the United Nations have included world cooperation in the solving of economic and social problems and, as we have seen, 'the promotion of social progress and better standards of life in larger freedom', was written into the Preamble to the Charter of the organisation as a solemn obligation resting on the member-nations. These pledges have not remained empty words. In the early years, United Nations action in the field of aid and development was centred largely in the Technical Assistance Programmes which, drawing on the pooled financial contributions of member-governments and utilising the various specialised bodies within the United Nations system, provided the technical experts, to whom we have already referred, and the supplies and equipment needed to enable receiving countries to make effective use of their services. In 1959, a United Nations Special Fund—a partnership in effect of more than a hundred governments and the whole range of Specialised Agencies—was created to encourage and finance in the preliminary stages, urgent development projects in the lowest-income range of countries. Seven years later, these two United Nations organisations were brought together in the single United Nations Development Programme which continues to operate, in the main, through the specialised bodies within the United Nations system. Meanwhile, the idea of a Development Decade had been launched in 1960 by the United Nations to dramatise the stark fact that the gap in resources between the modernised nations and the economically-backward countries was widening, leaving some two-thirds of humanity still below the poverty line. The Decade had as its twin goals, an annual average rate of growth in the total national income of the poorer countries of 5% and an increase in the amount of help given by the richer countries, so that this aid would amount to 1% of the combined national incomes of the richer states.

Trade as aid

Gradually, however, it was coming to be seen that though the developing countries would still require direct assistance from the richer countries, the greatest need was for them to be enabled to make their own economic way in the world by securing a larger share of international trade and by other measures designed to strengthen their economies. Only so, would they be able to reduce their dependence on foreign aid and reach a stage of economic independence comparable to the political independence they had already secured. With this goal in view, a United Nations Conference on Trade and Development attended by 122 nations, both rich and poor, which met in Geneva in 1964, adopted recommendations intended to protect the poorer nations from violent fluctuations in the world price of their primary products—cocoa, sugar, cotton, rubber, tea, tin, oilseeds and fats and so on—which form the bulk of their export trade, and to secure wider openings for their manufactured goods in the markets of the

The second World Development Conference opens in Delhi.

world. And as 1964 ended, the Conference was recognised as a permanent part of United Nations machinery in the economic field. Trade rather than aid became the slogan and the appeal of the developing world.

Four years later, in February 1968, a second World Conference on Trade and Development, attended this time by 133 states, met appropriately in New Delhi, the capital of India. Mrs Gandhi, Prime Minister of India, is seen presiding over the opening session in our photograph above. Its purpose in the cautious words of the Secretary-General of the United Nations, was

> to provide the opportunity for concerted practical action by the world community in a spirit of shared responsibility towards the achievement of common objectives, at least in the specific issues where concrete progress does not appear to be out of reach.

The common objectives had not, in fact, changed in the interval between the two Conferences; the major objective remained an improvement in their terms of trade for the developing countries so as to give them wider opportunities in the world's markets. But the problems which had pre-occupied the first Conference had, if anything, become more acute in the meantime and the prospect of reaching the declared goals had worsened. The poorer countries had gained little if any increased access to world markets; the quarter-share of world trade which they held in 1964 had, indeed, dwindled to a fifth by 1966. Moreover, though the volume of their exports had risen, sometimes quite sharply, the prices they received for them in world markets had steadily declined. One striking example can be quoted from the Haslemere Declaration, published in 1968 by a younger group among those professionally concerned with aid problems. It is taken from the experience of Ghana, two-thirds of whose export is cocoa. Between 1953 and 1961, export of cocoa from Ghana increased by 71% in volume but the income obtained from it increased by only 23%. Meanwhile, manufactured goods shipped to Ghana had gone up 11% in price which meant that a machine which cost Ghana the equivalent of 10 tons of cocoa in 1953, cost her 14 tons in 1961.

The New Delhi Conference did little to reverse these trends and on the whole disappointed the high hopes centred on it. The Conference was not a complete failure; the richer countries did undertake to try and increase the aid they give to the poorer countries by a quarter, and the resolutions of the Conference reaffirmed the intention of the donor countries to make a contribution of one per cent of their gross national product, the minimum target for foreign aid. But despite two months of debate; despite, to quote the calculations of one reporter, nearly a thousand meetings and twenty-eight million pages of documents, no agreements of substance were reached in Delhi and some important issues were not discussed at all.

Challenge to apathy
The rich world continues, therefore, to confront the poor world and the looming challenge of a world poverty crisis to order and to peace remains. U Thant has spoken of the urgent need for 'the industrialised countries to awaken from the apathy accompanying their affluence to the realities of the world around them.' 'We are now', he added 'near the point of no return.' The Secretary-General of the United Nations

Conferences on Trade and Development spoke of 'the very profound economic revolution' and 'the far-reaching transformation of the social structure' that has to take place in the developing world. This revolution he judged to be inevitable. We have to discuss, he said, not whether it is avoidable but 'what shape it must take, what degree of . . . social and political sacrifice, or moral sacrifice, this revolution of the Third World will entail'.

TOPICS FOR DISCUSSION

- What do you understand by the 'population explosion' and what kinds of action are needed to avert its dangers?

- If it is true that 'Charity begins at home', why should the richer nations help the poorer ones?

- Why is it important that the role of the United Nations, in promoting the economic and social development of the poorer countries, should be strengthened and extended?

4

Race and colour

We have seen that there is no sharply-defined frontier between the rich world and the poor world. The world poverty crisis is sometimes described as 'the North-South problem', to distinguish it from the so-called 'East-West problem', to which we later turn; and it is true, for the most part, that the poorer countries are to be found on or below the Equator and the richer countries in the Northern hemisphere. But poverty and acute human need dominate large parts of at least three continents and remedies impose responsibilities on rich and poor countries alike. A solution of the North-South problem is impossible, therefore, without action on a universal scale.

The conflict of race and colour is also international in its implications and presents as great a threat to a stable and peaceful world. But in geographical terms it is concentrated in more limited areas. There is no serious tension or conflict of a racial kind, at least between whites and non-whites, in Asia now that Western colonialism in most of that continent has come to an end. Race relations are not likely to become a grave problem within the countries of Australasia as long as they are able to maintain successfully their policy of excluding all but white immigrants from their shores, though there is some discrimination in Australia against the 1% of the population who are Aborigines. The United States has a race and colour problem of momentous importance for Americans, if not for the world at large, but it is essentially an American problem with, as yet, limited international repercussions.

In Africa, where the international clash of race and colour is mainly focused, there is no race problem of consequence, as far as black-white relationships are concerned, in the countries north of the Zambesi river which have become independent, and where power has passed to the African majority. These areas of central and northern Africa were always over-

47

Peoples of Africa : top, left : an Arab sailor in Mombasa ; below, left : a Ghanaian nurse in Kumasi ; top right : an Asian tailor ; below, right : a white farmer in Kenya

whelmingly black African areas in terms of population. Against an average ratio of 2·5 white Africans to every 100 black Africans for the whole of Africa, the ratio in Uganda, for example, is 1:700. In Nigeria it is 1:2,700. Moreover, many of the white people, who came to Africa north of the Zambesi, came as temporary residents intending to return home when their tasks as administrators, teachers, or businessmen were finished. Those who stayed after independence did so recognising that a new order had come into being and that they would have to stay, if at all, on its terms.

The race and colour problem in Africa is centred, therefore, in the main not in the new Africa of the black independent states but as the map on the next page shows in the four areas of the south where whites still hold preponderant power, that is in the Republic of South Africa, Rhodesia and the two major Portuguese colonies of Angola and Mozambique. The white people in these areas have vital common interests but, as countries, they are not alike. Their history and development has been different; their constitutional status varies. There are some differences in official attitudes within the four areas to the non-white majorities and in the ideas of white Africans as to the future development and destiny of their territories. Even so, pressures from black Africans and the wider world are bringing them closer together in a defensive unity and certain features characterise them all. In all these areas, power is effectively and, to all intents and purposes exclusively, in the hands of the white people; in all of them white supremacy is maintained by constitutional arrangements which deprive the black African majority of any significant political influence or by regulations and customs which discriminate against them and ensure their subordination to white interests.

The white southern Africans
To count heads alone is not, of course, to make an adequate appraisal of the problem centred in southern Africa or to reach a just and acceptable solution. Minorities also have their rights. But the minority status of the ruling white peoples is the basic reality of the situation in southern Africa and the facts can be briefly stated. The Republic of South Africa has a

Southern Africa : focus of the race problem

population of approximately 18·75 million. Of this some
3·5 million (about one-fifth of the population) are white;
1·8 million are the so-called Cape Coloured and about half a
million are Asian. The remaining 12–13 million (two-thirds
of the population) are black Africans. Of the white South
Africans, rather less than half are of Dutch ancestry with
some Huguenot stock; they speak Afrikaans and most of the

political as distinct from the economic power of the country is in their hands. The English-speaking white South Africans number 1·5 million and are mainly of British origin; their political influence steadily lessens but they still largely control the gold, uranium and diamond mines which are the principal source of the economic wealth of the country. The Cape Coloureds are people of mixed race descended from Hottentot Africans, imported slaves from East and West Africa and Europeans. The half-million Asians are the descendants of indentured workers who came originally from the Indian sub-continent, to work on the sugar plantations of Natal. The 12–13 million black South Africans are themselves divided into tribes of which the most numerous are the Xhosa, the Zulu and the Sotho, though all of them would want to be known simply as Africans or South Africans. Between 1951 and 1966 the total South African population increased by 25%. Within this overall figure, the white increase was 16%; the non-whites increased by percentages varying between 25 and 35%. By the year 2,000 the black African population of South Africa is likely to be more than twice what it is today—an estimated 33 million out of a total population of 42 million. The minority status of South Africans of European origin, becomes, that is to say, more pronounced every day.

The racial problem in Rhodesia is simpler since there are less than 4·75 million Rhodesians altogether. Of these, 4·5 million are black Rhodesians; most of the remainder, some 230,000, are white Rhodesians who in the main came originally from Britain, though with some additions from South Africa in recent times. The natural increase in the white population of Rhodesia is less than 2,500 a year; the natural increase among the black Rhodesians is seventy times as much. The black African population increases, in fact, every eighteen months by the total of the present white population.

The Portuguese colonies of Angola, Mozambique and Guinea have a total population of about 12 million of whom some 450,000 are Portuguese. There are substantially more white people in all these areas than there are in the black African states to the north but they are, in all cases, a decisive minority of the population. In South Africa the ratio of white people to black people is 1:4; in Rhodesia it is 1:18; in Angola 1:15; in Mozambique it is 1:35.

Safeguarding white supremacy

Political power, as we have said, is a preserve of the white people throughout southern Africa. In the Republic of South Africa white political supremacy has been reinforced by the abolition of even the limited political representation which the 40,000 male Coloured voters of Cape Province, who are of mixed racial origin, enjoyed under earlier constitutions. Now one race group is forbidden to interfere in the politics of another which means that political parties of mixed races are impossible. Membership in Parliament is limited to white South Africans and the arrangement under which for a time white senators were chosen to represent the black African millions came to an end in 1960. In this, as in other respects, full citizenship is denied to the black African, whatever his financial or economic status may be or his educational attainments.

In Rhodesia, some concession was made to the idea of a political partnership between the races in the Constitution of 1961 which gave black Africans for the first time some representation in the Rhodesian Parliament and the theoretical possibility of some real part in the business of government. But black Rhodesians on the two electoral lists established for them had to have substantial educational and property qualifications to exercise the vote and no serious inroad was made, or has yet been made, in the white monopoly of political power. It was the refusal of the white Rhodesians to offer any solid prospect of a growing participation for the black Rhodesians and ultimate majority power in the government of their country, which led to the conflict between the Rhodesian and British governments to which we later refer.

In the major Portuguese colonies or 'overseas provinces' of Angola and Mozambique, there is not even the semblance of democratic or representative institutions and the black Africans have no say or part in the government of the country. Sixty years ago the first tentative steps were taken in the direction of self-rule but the process was reversed when

Portugal itself became a dictatorship in 1926 and the same authoritarian principles were applied to the African provinces and to the homeland. The two territories are treated, in fact, as part of Portugal itself with power vested in local governors answerable directly to the government in Lisbon. There is little likelihood of any change in this situation until or unless a democratic system is re-established in Portugal itself.

Separating the races

In all the countries we are considering the white monopoly of political power is secured, not only by the formal denial of political rights to the black African, but also by a series of laws and regulations, based on race and colour, which, to a greater or less degree, are aimed at keeping the races apart and which apply to whites and non-whites alike. In the Republic of South Africa, the official policy of separate development (in Afrikaans, *apartheid*) is meant to be carried to its logical end in the series of Bantustans or exclusively black African areas, where local government is in black African hands and foreign policy, defence, the police and the courts administered by the central South African government. This policy, if fully carried out, would in effect convert South Africa into a two-nation country; under this system white people would be gradually excluded from the Bantustans and the black Africans would become foreigners in status in white South Africa. The process has gone much more slowly than was intended and so has the economic development of the Bantustans already planned or formed. The only fully-established Bantustan is the Greater Transkei which is an area twice as large as Wales, lying between Natal and Cape Province. But other Bantustans have been started in Zululand, the Northern Transvaal and in the Ovambaland tribal territories of South-West Africa.

In any case, these all-black areas absorb little more than a third of the black South African population and the proportion tends to decrease rather than increase. The rest of the black Africans remain in areas reserved for white South Africans, living in townships close to but separated from the industrial centres where they are employed. Black Africans

At home in Soweto township

employed on European farms do live on the farmland, each tribe having its own special area, and throughout the country one black African servant is allowed to live with a white family employing him. But in general, in South African areas reserved for white South Africans, the principle of segregation or separation is strictly applied to all racial groups. White and non-white people may not travel in the same buses and rail coaches or eat in the same restaurants or use cinemas at the same time as white South Africans and use the same toilet facilities or play football together. They may not sit on the same benches or use the same recreation centres and public beaches; they may not make love together or marry; they cannot be educated together except in one or two institutions of higher education. All South African citizens must possess an identity card which gives their classification according to race but black South Africans must also have a reference book which not only gives detailed information about the holder

Apartheid in operation

but also records his comings and goings and so controls his movements from area to area. The whole system is enforced by stern police action which, in 1968, resulted in the prosecution of nearly 2,000 black Africans per day for violations of the various regulations, including even the accidental misplacing of reference books. 'A terrible feeling of insecurity', said a special report on South Africa in *The Economist*, 'is being thrust down on the urban African.'

Perhaps the Cape Coloureds, the people, that is, of mixed racial origin, have had the roughest deal of all in South Africa. They have not only lost the restricted political rights they used to have, but they do not even have the prospect of the limited self-government offered to the blacks in the Bantustans. They have no security in business or urban house tenure. They cannot attend concerts, theatres or cinemas with the white community. They can only look forward, as a report of the British Council of Churches put it, 'to a second-class citizenship for themselves and their children; a citizenship of decreasing value with every new addition of traditional Coloured jobs to those reserved for white persons.'

The Rhodesian problem

The white government of Rhodesia is not, as yet, so decisively committed, as is the South African government, to the policy of *apartheid*; though current official policy would seem designed to perpetuate white minority rule indefinitely, some white Rhodesians would be ready to envisage an eventual partnership in government of both black and white citizens, and some would be ready to see the country handed over to black majority rule in the fullness of time. Meanwhile, nearly all black Rhodesians are denied the vote; the various Land Apportionment Acts divide the cultivatable land between the two races in such a way as to reserve the best agricultural areas, and almost half the total land area of the country, for the white minority. The effective separation of the races is achieved by broadly the same customs and methods as in South Africa. The black Rhodesians live in townships on the outskirts of the city centres; there are separate schools, hotels and restaurants for their use and separate entrances for the two races to public buildings and post offices. In Salisbury, the capital, for example, no black Rhodesian may own property though the life of the city is largely kept going by black Rhodesian labour.

Conditions in Portuguese Africa are scarcely comparable since Portuguese attitudes to race relations and Portuguese methods of administration differ so widely from those that obtain in the other areas. Black Africans are, in fact, made subject to disciplines harsher than those practised in the rest of Southern Africa, with the result that the masses are unusually docile and the growth of nationalistic sentiment has been forestalled. A B.B.C. commentator who visited Angola in 1969, described the province as a striking exception in an age of decolonisation; it was a system still of pure colonisation. It was still regarded, he said, by the Portuguese settlers as a 'land of opportunity' even if to settle there meant 'living in an often beleaguered atmosphere of a pioneering frontier'. The Portuguese thought it valuable enough to keep there fifty thousand armed men with the difficult job of policing a vast area, now constantly under attack by Freedom Fighters or terrorists. Despite the fact that it is 'a carefully stratified society' he found far fewer racial barriers than in South Africa and Rhodesia. Africans could, and sometimes did, get 'top jobs'. He added, surprisingly, that Portuguese Angola could be 'the cradle of a multi-racial society'. There was already a 'great deal of free and easy mixing, particularly among the younger people.'

The 'white' point of view

Inevitably in these circumstances the governing white minorities in southern Africa are the target of world-wide opposition and condemnation. They come under attack not only from black nationalists (mostly in exile) from their own countries and from the black African States to the north but also from world opinion focused in the United Nations. So deep is the feeling created by the policies and practices of the white southern Africans that little effort is made to try and understand the motives that inspire them and the dilemmas they have to face. The white peoples of southern Africa, especially in South Africa and Rhodesia, are not temporary sojourners in a strange land which they eventually plan to leave. Their forebears came to what is now South Africa three centuries ago, at about the same time as the black African Bantus moved in from the north. Angola has been administered by the Portuguese since 1500 and Mozambique since 1505. The earliest British settlers went to Rhodesia eighty or ninety years ago. Most South Africans, and not a few Rhodesians, have known no other home. Driven from southern Africa, they would have no natural home elsewhere. It is true that they could not have achieved what they have achieved in material terms without the cheap labour of the black African or without the foreign capital attracted from abroad. But their energy and enterprise have built these countries, and especially South Africa, into modern communities providing not only prosperity for the white people

but material and cultural standards for the South African
Bantu far in advance of the standards of living enjoyed
by black Africans elsewhere. The South Africans claim, for
example, that four out of every five of their Bantus between the
age of seven and twenty-one, are already literate compared
with a general figure of one in five in the rest of Africa.
Despite repression and restriction there is, in fact, a steady
in-flow of black Africans into the Republic of South Africa
from other African states. It is not surprising, therefore, that
facing a rising tide of nationalism in continental Africa and
fearful that they will have no worthwhile future in a predomi-
nantly black South Africa, the white people set up defensive
barriers to protect and preserve the material standards and
cultural achievements of the country and its people. Self-
interest and self-protection inspire the white southern
African, but, seeing the chaos and confusion into which some
of the independent black African states have fallen from time
to time, he can claim with some reason that he is preserving
for all southern Africans, white or black, an area of stability
and peace in a troubled continent and a restless world.

The 'white' dilemma

None of these claims can be lightly dismissed and no
solution of the race and colour problem in southern Africa
which ignores the sentiment and interests of the white people,
can be peacefully or justly achieved, or be expected to endure,
if achieved. It is just possible that a future could be built for
South Africa, in particular, on the basis of 'separate and equal
development' for the black and the white races if the policy
could be consistently applied and the separation—and the
equality—were made complete. To say, 'Go away and be free
somewhere else' to the black African, might make sense if
those who said it really wanted him to go. The fact is that the
economic life and wealth of the country, and the prosperity
of the whites themselves, is largely dependent on the plentiful
supply of black African labour close to the centres of industry,
and this dependence is increasing rather than decreasing.
The South African Trade Union Council calculates that the
black African labour force in manufacturing will amount to

80% of the total by 1971. This is the crucial dilemma facing the white South African. He wants, because he cannot do without it, the labour of the black South African, but he does not want to live with him in the only kind of inter-racial relationship within a country, which is morally tolerable in the world of today. The *Rand Daily Mail*, a South African newspaper, pointing out that South Africa must choose between the integration or the separation of the races, went on to say:

> We cannot bring ourselves to accept the logical consequences of either course. There is a dilemma of unacceptable alternatives. As a nation, we have lost our way because we are afraid to follow the logical path in either direction. . . . We are trying to enjoy the benefits of economic integration while refusing the discomforts of social and political integration.

The dilemma is a real one and easy to resolve only for those who do not have to face it directly. But the fundamental weakness of the white minorities in southern Africa is that they are trying to maintain systems of government, based on a principle of racial discrimination which is now repugnant to the bulk of the civilised world, and is a direct denial of international obligations embodied in the Charter of the United Nations and in the United Nations' Universal Declaration of Human Rights. The principle is equally repugnant, let it be said, to certain sections of opinion in South Africa itself, as witness a statement made by the South African Council of Churches in September, 1968, branding the doctrine of racial separation as 'a false faith . . . truly hostile to Christianity.' Even if all the member-states in the United Nations were not required by the Charter to repudiate the racial policies of the governments concerned, it is inconceivable that the non-white African world would sit idly by while principles of white supremacy remain entrenched in the southern states of the African continent. The black races in Africa are rapidly becoming politically conscious. They are 'getting to their feet', as Lord Ritchie-Calder once expressed it, 'determined to confront their fellow human beings on equal terms.' Over large areas of Africa governing power is already in their hands. Their responsible leaders might be willing to share power with the white peoples in South Africa and Rhodesia under some form of racial partnership. They will never accept that, in these areas, the abhorred system of white minority rule should continue for ever. No issue touches them more deeply than this. 'For the best part of four centuries', wrote Canon Max Warren, 'as the coloured races see it, the white man has been on the attack. What we are seeing today is the counter-attack.' The counter-attack will be pressed relentlessly against the white regimes in the south by black Africans outside southern Africa, even if the average black African in the south shows no eagerness to be 'liberated', as a recent British journalistic visitor put it 'by the peoples of the Congo and Ethiopia whose incomes per head are a fraction of his own.'

The United Nations takes a hand

The counter-attack began, in fact, in an overwhelmingly white United Nations in the earliest days of the world organisation. The Preamble to the Charter reaffirmed the faith of 'We the peoples', for whom it claimed to speak, 'in fundamental human rights and the dignity and worth of the human person.' Article 55(c) of the Charter itself requires the United Nations 'to promote universal respect for and observance of human rights and fundamental freedoms for all without distinction as to race, sex, language, or religion.' The Universal Declaration of Human Rights, adopted in 1948, set out in thirty articles the basic rights and freedoms to which all men and women everywhere are declared to be entitled. Article 2 laid down that: 'Everyone is entitled to all the rights and freedoms set forth in this Declaration without distinction of any kind, such as race, colour, sex, language, religion, politics or other opinion, national or social origin, property, birth or other status.'

These statements and the commitments they involve, made it inevitable that from the outset, the United Nations would find itself in conflict with the white regimes of southern Africa and the racial policies they pursue. For some few states-members of the organisation, including France, these were matters of domestic responsibility for the countries concerned, in which the United Nations had no right to interfere. For the majority, they were essentially matters of international responsibility threatening or likely to threaten world peace and security, which it was impossible for the United Nations to disregard. In resolution after resolution from 1948 onwards, the General Assembly condemned the policies of *apartheid*, demanded their abandonment by the South African government and insisted on the legal right of the international community through the United Nations, to supervise and, if need be, criticise South African administration of the former German colony of South-West Africa which first came under South African control by mandate of the League of Nations in 1920. (The Mandates system of the League put all the former colonies of the defeated Germans and Japanese under the control of various victors in the First World War, pending the ability of these areas to govern themselves.) Successive South African governments from 1945 onwards, rejected all these claims on the grounds that both the internal situation in South Africa, and South African administration of South-West Africa, were exclusively their business and no-one else's. They refused all admittance to investigating delegations and Commissions representing the United Nations.

This confrontation between South Africa and the United Nations began when there were only four African States-members of the United Nations, one of them South Africa itself. It was intensified from 1960 onwards, when the admission of new members brought a large number of independent black African states into the world organisation. Under pressures from a Special Committee on Non-self-governing Territories, which had been set up in 1961 to encourage rapid progress towards self-rule in areas still under foreign control, the General Assembly sharpened its opposition to white South African policies and brought the self-governing and semi-independent Rhodesia for the first time within the scope of its concerns. Annual resolutions of the Assembly called for elections on a universal franchise in Rhodesia and demanded a new constitution opening up the prospect of ultimate majority rule for the four million black Rhodesians. Following the Unilateral Declaration of Independence in 1965, made by the white government of Rhodesia, which put that government in rebellion against the British Crown and Parliament, the United Nations at the insistence of Great Britain began the process of applying economic pressures or sanctions against Rhodesia, in the hope of persuading the white Rhodesians to reach a settlement of the Rhodesian question on principles acceptable to the United Nations and world opinion. Sanctions had not yet been applied to the Republic of South Africa, but in November 1966, the General Assembly having failed to persuade the South African Government to recognise the responsibility of the United Nations for South-West Africa, formally ended the mandate of the South African government over South-West Africa and, on paper, transferred responsibility for the administration of the territory from the Republic of South Africa to the United Nations itself. In November 1968 the General Assembly adopted a resolution calling for the extension of comprehensive and compulsory sanctions to South Africa with a view to compelling its Government to accept and carry out the decisions of the United Nations.

The United Nations' dilemma

There are dilemmas in this southern African situation not only for the white regimes, and especially the government in South Africa, but also for the international community represented by the United Nations. The United Nations has the duty to voice the conscience of the world on situations and policies which challenge vital principles of its Charter and of its Universal Declaration of Human Rights. It has the duty beyond this, to take such action as may persuade the ruling regimes in southern Africa to change their racial policies and make possible some peaceful settlement of the problem. If it fails in these tasks, it risks the break-up of the United Nations itself; it encourages more militant black Africans to take the law into their own hands and the communist great powers to aid and abet them in so doing. It makes possible, if not certain, assuming no peaceful solution is found, an eventual racial war in Africa which, as we have said, could set the world ablaze.

This is one horn of the dilemma; the other is that the

United Nations can only enforce its aims and its will in southern Africa, in face of the non-cooperation of the white regimes, by measures which threaten to bring the world organisation into ultimate military conflict with the countries concerned. Economic pressure against Rhodesia can not be made fully effective without the cooperation of South Africa and failing that cooperation, without economic pressure against South Africa itself. Economic pressure against South Africa—difficult in any case for a country like Great Britain with an economy closely bound to the economy of South Africa—can scarcely be made effective without consequent risk of a naval and military confrontation between South Africa and the great powers, who are alone capable of carrying out, for example, a naval blockade of the ports of South Africa in the name of the United Nations. Meanwhile the effect of all the international pressure exerted against the white southern Africans, has been to unite them more closely to each other and to their governments and to stiffen their resistance.

No simple solution

No simple or speedy solution of this problem of race and colour is possible therefore whether it is seen as a 'domestic' issue in a given country such as the United States or as an international problem centred in the southern half of Africa and involving the political and moral responsibility of the United Nations. On the face of it, no compromises seem possible; world opinion will increasingly condemn entrenched systems of racial discrimination wherever they may appear; the white regimes on the other hand will not readily or ever— without the most cast-iron safeguards—submit their fate and future to the hazards and uncertainties of black majority rule. It is just possible that the growing economic interdependence of the countries of Africa—north and south—might encourage them to work out a policy of peaceful coexistence with each other.

But there is not unlimited time. President Kaunda of Zambia, speaking in London in 1968, ventured the opinion that the world was heading for a tragedy in southern Africa, a conflict of interests that could lead to such serious bloodshed

Botswana becomes independent : the Duchess of Kent reads a message from the Queen.

'as to make Vietnam look like child's play.' Four years earlier, the Secretary-General of the United Nations addressing the Algerian National Assembly said:

> There is the clear prospect that racial conflict, if we cannot avert or finally eliminate it, will grow into a destructive monster . . . which will eat away the possibilities of good, of all that mankind has hitherto achieved, and reduce men to the lowest and most bestial levels of intolerance and hatred. This, for the sake of all our children, whatever their race or colour, must not be permitted to happen.

TOPICS FOR DISCUSSION

- Why is there a 'race problem' in Africa, but not to any serious extent in other continents—apart from North America?

- Do you understand the attitude on racial questions of the white peoples and governments of southern Africa and do you see any solid justification for it?

- Do you believe that the United Nations should, if necessary, use force against the white governments of southern Africa to make them change their attitudes and their policies on the race problem?

5

Russia and the West

The East-West problem, as we are accustomed to call it, raises the third and last of the issues on which the future of peace and international order largely depends. The label is convenient but in a sense misleading, since the words East and West, used in this context, indicate not geography but politics and ideology. In the realm of systems and ideas what is at issue is the world-wide conflict between liberal democracy on the one hand and international communism on the other. In political and more practical terms what is involved is the relationship between Western Europe and North America, on the one hand and Eastern Europe, on the other.

Twenty years ago this would have been seen as the main source of international tension and the likeliest ground for a third world war. It would have been then described in simple and broadly accurate terms, as a confrontation between the communist and non-communist worlds. The Soviet Union was the acknowledged leader of a bloc of communist states which included the People's Republic of China and the smaller communist states of Eastern Europe—Hungary, Poland, Albania, Bulgaria, Czechoslovakia, Rumania and the Soviet zone of East Germany which later became the German Democratic Republic. Yugoslavia, though still a communist country, had already achieved a measure of independence from the Soviet Union after its quarrel with Stalin but all the others were under the undisputed dominance of Moscow. Similarly on the non-communist side, the alliance of the Western great powers—France, Britain and the United States—together with such countries as Turkey, Greece, Canada, Norway, Italy and West Germany, acknowledged the leadership of the United States, though the West was never a tightly disciplined group of states as were the states of the Eastern bloc. This was the heyday of the cold war to which we referred in our opening chapter, the period of consistent and often bitter hostility between the two 'worlds' and of what appeared to be the unbreakable unity of each of the two camps.

This unity has now been broken on both sides, so that it is no longer accurate to speak of two worlds that are bound to collide with each other or to use the simple formula East-West, in parallel with Rich-Poor or North-South. Soviet overlordship of the communist world has been challenged by China and to a degree, as we shall see, by some of the smaller European countries of the communist group. On the other hand American leadership of the Western Alliance—the North Atlantic Treaty Organisation as it is formally called—has been challenged by France and in general the influence of the United States in the West has tended to diminish. But there has not only been change in the balance of power within each bloc. On the communist side, some significant domestic changes have taken place in the Soviet Union itself and a growing independence from Moscow on the part of some of the smaller communist countries in Eastern Europe, has gone hand in hand with changes in their internal systems and in their relations with the non-communist states of the West.

Three aspects

The East-West problem is not then what it was in 1950. Today we have to see it, if not as three problems, at least as a problem with three aspects each interacting on the other, it is true, but distinct to a degree and requiring distinct responses from the western world. Western relations with Soviet Russia are one thing; with the People's Republic of China they are another; with the smaller communist states of Europe something different still. We devote a separate chapter to the immensely important problem of the future role of China and of her relationship with the Western world. Here we look at Soviet-Western relations primarily and, within this context, at the role of the smaller communist countries of Eastern Europe now beginning to emerge tentatively from tutelage to Soviet Russia.

Winston Churchill once described Soviet Russia as 'a riddle wrapped in an enigma'. No unravelling of the enigma and no understanding of Soviet actions and attitudes today, is possible without some knowledge of the basic facts of Russian geography and history. Save for what has been called the peninsula of Western Europe, Russia occupies almost the whole of the Eurasian continent, the largest land mass in the world. In Russia, there is the immense plain of Central and Northern Asia, an area almost devoid of the natural frontiers which might have served for its defence. So throughout its history, Russia has been invaded repeatedly by its neighbours. The Mongol invasion of the thirteenth century under Ghenghis Khan, which was not the first invasion of the country from the East, subjected Russia to a ruthless Tartar domination lasting for two centuries. From the early seventeenth century onwards, the attacks came from the West. Five times between 1610 and 1941, Russia was overrun by Western armies, for example the armies of Charles XII of Sweden, of Napoleon and Hitler, which moved towards her across the open plains of Eastern Europe. The Russians have experienced, to quote Louis Halle—'ten centuries of constant, mortal fear.' Fear became and perhaps remains, as Halle puts it: 'the prime driving force in Russia, the principal reason for the organisation and expansion of Russian society.'

This gives us a clue to much that is otherwise obscure and perplexing about Russia and Russian attitudes to the outside world. Faced with successive onslaughts from their enemies, the Russians came to accept the centralised government of Moscow and the autocratic rule of the Tsars as the price of their survival. The Kremlin, which lies in the very heart of Moscow, became the symbol of the 'fortress-mentality' which still, to a degree, governs Russian outlook and behaviour. Fear of yet more attacks, led the rulers of Russia to seek security by extending the frontiers of their country and pushing further away from them, as they judged, the threat of renewed invasion. Moreover, the distrust of foreigners resulting from repeated aggressions against them, led the Russians to favour a closely-knit, secretive and even conspiratorial kind of society which the foreigner would find it hard to penetrate and which, in essence, remains to this day.

Lenin addresses the revolutionary armies, Moscow 1919.

The experience of constant invasion had one further consequence for the Russians. Arnold Toynbee points out that all
the defeats or invasions, some of which were successfully
repulsed, that the Russians suffered at Western hands over
three centuries, were the result of the superiority in inventive-
ness and technological skills of the West. From Peter the
Great onwards, the leaders of Russia sought to offset this
inferiority and to carry out a technological revolution of their
own. Their achievements in the field of space exploration
are a symbol of the success they have had in one aspect of
technological development though it is a success obtained at
the cost of a continuing backwardness in other fields.

The communists take over

The characteristic then of Russian society and of Russian
reactions to the outside world, were fixed long before the
communist revolution of 1917, and in a fundamental sense
have remained unchanged to this day. Much in Soviet
behaviour that we attribute to communism is a reflection of
these deeper Russian influences. The communist revolution
was not and could not be a clean break with the past. The
communist leadership of Russia after 1917 altered little,
despite its revolutionary zeal. There was certainly no radical
change in the nature of Russian government. Communist

dictatorship replaced Tsarist dictatorship; one authoritarian system replaced another. There was no change in the distrust which the Russians felt for the outside world or in the secrecy with which they sought to hide all their own actions and intentions. There was no change in the determination of the 'new' Russia to achieve security by advancing its frontiers as far as possible towards the West. But the communist leadership, especially under Stalin, brought to all these aims a ruthlessness and an efficiency which had not been known under the Tsars.

Stalin's long reign of thirty years as undisputed dictator, was one long process of sharpening all these weapons for use against possible enemies inside and outside the confines of Russia. The secret police were used to carry out the un-questioned will of the dictator; the richer Russian peasants who actively resisted the enforced collectivisation of their farms, were liquidated in their thousands. All semblance of opposition or dissent was suppressed and potential rivals for power were destroyed in a series of massive purges which are believed to have cost twelve million lives. Determined to ensure that Soviet Russia would not fall before a new enemy, as Imperial Russia had collapsed before the Kaiser's armies in 1917, Stalin speeded up the technological revolution begun by his predecessors. The Soviet Union, as he saw it, must become a truly modern industrial state equipped to meet the rest of the world on its own terms. It must eventually become equal, if not superior, to the greatest of all powers, the United States. Everything therefore, including the immediate well-being of the Russian masses, was sacrificed under his rule to the building-up of industrial strength and the capacity of the Soviet Union to hold its own against the advanced countries of the West. Stalin made unlimited demands on the Russian people. His cruel and arrogant assumption was that, where he chose to lead them, they would follow.

Fear and counter-fear
From the beginning, the Bolshevik or communist revolution in Russia was recognised, both by those who welcomed it and those who did not, as an event of historic importance but

it had to make its way against lukewarm, if not hostile, world opinion. The Western allies of the First World War, seeking to offset the military advantage to the Germans of the Russian withdrawal from the war, and fearful of the spread of revolutionary ideas to their own countries, launched a counter-revolutionary war against the new leaders of Russia. They lost their war; the counter-revolution failed and the communist state survived, but the circle of fear and counter-fear was enlarged. The net result was an intensification of mutual fears and a strengthening of the suspicious and defensive attitudes of the new Russia. The Soviet regime was 'sent to Coventry' diplomatically by many states. Britain recognised the regime diplomatically at an early stage, but sixteen years were to elapse before the Russian communists gained diplomatic recognition from the United States. The Soviet Union was too busy in these earlier days consolidating the revolution and repairing its economic weaknesses to take any significant part in the councils of the world. But it was already clear that the new Russia, as she grew in strength and influence, was bound to become an uncomfortable bedfellow for the established countries of the West.

In 1940, when the West was already at war with Nazi Germany, Stalin made an alliance of convenience with the Nazi leaders which he hoped might keep Russia out of the Second World War. The bid failed. Within two years the pact was destroyed by Hitler's invasion of the Soviet Union—a further and, to date, final invasion from the West. The Soviet Union, also for convenience, was thrown into an alliance with the Western powers against the common enemy—Nazism. The alliance lasted long enough to ensure the military defeat of Hitler but within two years of the ending of the war the alliance fell apart, broken on the conflicting interests of the partners and their conflicting views as to the kind of peace they were determined to secure. The cold war, to which we referred in our first chapter, began in earnest.

The intensive phase of this war between the U.S.S.R., and the Western powers was to last until the death of Stalin in 1953. The first battlefield—literally so in this case—was in Korea, where the United States in the name of the United

'Cold War' at the United Nations : Andrei Vyshinsky holds the floor.

Nations was defending South Korea against aggression from North Korea, which was in communist hands. Basically in American eyes, this was a war fought to prevent the spread of communism in Asia. Soviet armies were not involved but Soviet political diplomacy fought a bitter and unrelenting war of propaganda around the world against the United States, designed to obstruct American aims and lend aid and comfort to the North Koreans. This was the time when the Soviet spokesman, Vyshinsky, brought to the defence of Soviet policy in the United Nations the same fierce and ruthless advocacy that he had used as Stalin's chief prosecutor in the State 'trials' in which Stalin organised the merciless liquidation of his domestic opponents. It was the period when, within the United Nations, the communist bloc spoke with one voice—the voice of Stalin and the Soviet Union and voted unanimously on all issues as the Soviet Union dictated. According to this unanimous, and often unscrupulous propaganda, the West and especially the United States, were 'the aggressive instigators of a new war'; the Soviet Union and its friends, the undisputed 'champions of peace'. The war was a two-way affair to some extent; the West reacted with a counter-propaganda and the setting-up of a Western defensive alliance to counteract the solidarity of the communist bloc. But the pace and intensity of the cold war was set by the Russians, and their energy and influence sustained it.

The death of Stalin

So it was to be until March 1953 when Stalin died, an event which marks a kind of watershed in the post-war history of Soviet Russia and in her relations with the outside world. Following a speech, delayed for three years, by the then Soviet leader Khrushchev, denouncing Stalin and repudiating his crimes, Stalin's body was taken from the Mausoleum in the Red Square of Moscow, where it had lain side by side with the body of Lenin, the founder of the Soviet State, and interred in humbler ground beneath the Kremlin wall. The process of 'de-Stalinisation', as it was called, within Russia began its slow and uneven course. Recognising that the Soviet people could not for ever be denied the fruits of their labours and the material benefits of the forty-year-old revolution, the Russian leaders shifted gears, as it were, in their economic policy so that an increasing consideration for the Russian as consumer, could improve the day-to-day living standards of the people. Centralised control from Moscow was loosened to a degree, and more economic authority given to the sixteen separate Republics of the U.S.S.R. and to individual industries. The pressure of the secret police was relaxed, though not entirely removed, and the population of the forced labour camps which had been the instruments, other than outright liquidation, of Stalin's tyranny, reduced. More attention was paid to the legal rights of the Soviet citizen, embodied long enough in the Constitution, but invariably disregarded. A process of rehabilitation was used to restore the reputation, but not the lives, of a selected few of Stalin's leading victims. Internationally the Russian leaders, recognising that Stalin's policy of uncompromising non-cooperation was paying no dividends for Russia herself, began to moderate the temper of their speeches and postures within the United Nations, and to acknowledge the value of limited agreements on marginal disarmament measures with the Western powers. 'The cold war' was not called off altogether, but henceforth it was to be fought at less frigid temperatures.

In general, this is the picture of the changed, and changing, Russia that we see today. The trends we have referred to, have broadly continued; Russia has become an easier country to live in; the life of the Soviet people has grown steadily more normal (as normality would be understood in the countries of the West). Some limited expressions of criticism, and even of public protest, were permitted and even encouraged for a time if they referred to the Stalinist past. Contacts at the cultural and tourist level between the Soviet Union and the Western world have been allowed to expand modestly. It even became possible in 1967, to buy other than communist newspapers from the West in the streets of Moscow. But fearful lest this freedom should begin to challenge the Communist Party's monopoly of power and their own authority, the Soviet leaders have, from time to time, sharply applied the brakes to this process of controlled liberalisation and have imposed, as

*Rulers of Russia: President Podgorny, Defence Minister Grechko,
Party Secretary Brezhnev and Premier Kosygin, in the Red Square*

the treatment in recent times of some Soviet writers and their
sympathisers have shown, severe if not savage punishments
on those who demanded a fuller creative freedom for themselves and others. There are still tens of thousands of political
prisoners, including religious and other prisoners of conscience, in Soviet jails. The Soviet Union remains, therefore, a
totalitarian state based on the dictatorship of the Communist
Party, whose membership covers only two per cent of the
230 million Russian people, and a country still largely resistant
to the democratic tendencies which have revealed themselves
elsewhere. Further reluctant concessions to freedom may be
made in the Soviet Union as time goes on, but as long as the
communist monopoly of government and of power remains,
no marked or decisive change is likely in the pattern of life of
the Soviet people or in the official relations of Russia with the
world outside and with the West in particular.

Internationally, as we have seen, the Soviet Union is
obliged to avoid the extreme clash of policies with the West
that might result in thermo-nuclear war between the great
powers. Because of trends that are irresistible in the longer

run in any country in the modern world, the Soviet rulers are likely to have to give increasing priority, not to vague revolutionary aims but to the national interests of the Soviet state and the need to improve the lot of the Soviet people. Beyond this there is a growing, though not always openly acknowledged, community of interest between the two superpowers—the United States and the Soviet Union; a recognition that their problems are in many ways similar and their destinies bound to be more closely intertwined. All these are factors that could tend to improve the Soviet Union's relations with the United States and the West in general, though, as the crisis in 1968 over Czechoslovakia demonstrated, the Soviet rulers are prepared to endanger those relations in face of a possible crumbling-away of the European communist bloc and the threat this might present to their authority within the Soviet Union itself. But even if the general trend is for Soviet Russia to improve her relations with the West, it is by the same token a trend which may well tend to deepen her quarrel with Mao's China and present her therefore with an uncomfortable and difficult choice. If she moves deliberately towards 'stability' and better relations with the West, she risks losing more of her influence in world revolutionary movements to the Chinese.

Russia's client states

The death of Stalin opened a new phase not only in the Soviet Union but also in communist Eastern Europe outside Russia. Stalin's despotism had embraced not only his own country but, in effect, all the smaller countries of Eastern Europe in which, after the defeat of Hitler, local communists with the backing of Soviet Russia and the Red Army, had seized or taken over power. Governments obedient to Stalin and his aims, were established in all the countries concerned; the political line they followed was indistinguishable from Stalin's; their economies were integrated with those of Soviet Russia in the primary interest, not of their own people, but of the Soviet state. In three of the countries, revolt against Stalinist domination came at an early stage. In 1948, Tito's successful resistance to Stalin's dictates enabled Yugoslavia to assume an independent role and to renounce the pacts which governed the military and economic relations of the communist countries. In 1956, a peaceful revolt of the Polish people removed the Stalinist leaders of Poland and gave Poland—uncomfortably close as she is to Soviet Russia and closely dependent on her—a somewhat less oppressive regime, though the early hopes that Poland might progress steadily from this point to still greater freedom have not been realised. The same year, the Hungarian people's demand for a greater measure of national independence provoked Soviet military intervention and the bloody suppression of Hungary's bid for greater freedom by Soviet tanks and guns. In 1953, an attempt by the workers of the Soviet-controlled Eastern zone of Germany to gain more freedom, was also forcibly suppressed by the use of Soviet military power.

The thaw spreads

The consequences of the death of Stalin which resulted in a modest liberalisation within Russia itself began, in time, to make themselves felt in the smaller communist-controlled states. Soviet Russia maintains an iron control over East Germany and no liberalising tendency has been allowed to appear. In Albania, the Stalinist-type leaders fell out with the new Soviet leaders and transferred their political and ideological loyalties to Mao's China. Bulgaria, like other East European countries, began for economic reasons to foster tourist trade with the West but remained within a close political relationship with the U.S.S.R. Hungary similarly developed its tourist industry and cautiously extended its cultural contacts with the West but its government, like that of Bulgaria and Poland, remained staunchly linked politically with the Soviet Union and like them, cooperated with the U.S.S.R. in the invasion and occupation of Czechoslovakia in August, 1968.

It was in Rumania and Czechoslovakia that the pressures to free themselves from the tight political control of Soviet Russia and generally to assert their national independence, were most strongly felt and expressed, though earlier in Rumania than in Czechoslovakia. In 1967 Rumania, while maintaining her strict internal communist system, created a precedent by entering into diplomatic relations with West Germany and further developed her independence in foreign policy and her trading and cultural links with the West. She did not join in the action taken against the Czechoslovaks by Russia and her allies. Early in 1968, the new Communist leadership in Czechoslovakia set in train economic and political changes intended to remove the more repressive aspects of government and to create in the words of one of its leaders, Mr. Dubcek: 'a free, modern and truly humane society'. A few months later the Soviet Union, fearful for the effect of these changes on its own internal and external security, militarily occupied Czechoslovak cities and countryside and forced the Czechoslovak authorities to suspend, if not to abandon, many of the measures which had given the Czechoslovak people at least a glimpse of greater freedom. This ruthless intervention, undertaken with some military support from Bulgaria, Hungary, Poland and East Germany, earned the condemnation not only of non-Communist world opinion but of Communists themselves in several countries.

The Czechoslovak crisis illustrated the dilemma facing some and, in time, probably all the smaller communist countries of Eastern Europe. They want to be independent states able to decide their own policies and actions according to their national interests. They do not necessarily want to renounce Communism and certainly not to return to the reactionary political systems of their past. They are fully aware of the international facts of life and of the close economic and political ties which bind them to the Soviet Union. But they do want to develop their socialism in their own way and to give it what they call 'a more human face'. The dilemma of their communist rulers is that if they move too quickly in this direction they provoke the fears and hostility of the Soviet Union; if they move too slowly, they may create internal pressures which they cannot control.

The invasion of Czechoslovakia in August 1968, by the Soviet Union and its four accomplices, not only damaged the reputation of the Soviet Union throughout the world but proved a severe set-back to the confidence and cooperation between the great powers of East and West which had been slowly growing in recent years and on which the future of world peace must largely depend. It was never likely that the Soviet occupation of Czechoslovakia would lead to immediate or early military conflict between the Soviet Union and the West. But the crisis made it disturbingly clear that in their fear of freedom, there is virtually no limit to the steps the Soviet leaders are prepared to take to suppress movements towards freedom in Eastern Europe which might sooner or later extend to their own territories and people. It also made clear that there can be no true and stable peace in Europe and the world, unless and until Soviet Russia has achieved more internal freedom for itself and become ready to grant it to others.

TOPICS FOR DISCUSSION

- Would you think that the Russian Revolution of 1917 marked a real 'turning-point in history'—and, if so, for what reasons?

- How far is it true to say that the United States and Soviet Russia have common problems and common interests? Can you see these becoming a real safeguard of peace in the world?

- Did the military occupation of Czechoslovakia in 1968, by the Soviet Union and its four allies, increase or diminish the dangers of world war?

6

China and the world

We have suggested that, perhaps, the greatest danger to peace in Europe lies in the loosening-up of the Soviet empire in Eastern Europe, of which the events in Czechoslovakia in the summer of 1968 were a portent and a sign. A rapid and successful challenge to Soviet overlordship in what it regards as its sphere of influence in Eastern Europe, might create a situation in which the Soviet Union and the West were brought into open conflict with each other. But it is not the deliberate will of either side that this should happen and both sides have compelling reasons to do their best to ensure that the clash does not come. Despite the uncertainties, there is little fear in the Western nations of a direct attack upon themselves from the Soviet Union nor in the Soviet Union of an assault from the West. The problem in Europe is how to reconcile the extension of freedom in the communist countries of Eastern Europe with the maintenance of peace.

There is no reason, either, to assume a military clash between China and the West, or for that matter between China and the Soviet Union; but here the uncertainties are even greater. The third of the world's people who live in China, including their rulers, have little or no contact with the outside world. China has no seat in the United Nations and whatever attractions she may have for the revolutionary-minded the world over, she plays little or no direct part as yet in world affairs. The direction which her own communist revolution is to take, is still unsure. But she is already on the way to becoming a fully-fledged nuclear power, possessing the most advanced nuclear weapons and the capacity to deliver them. She takes her cue from the saying of her leader Mao Tse-tung, that 'power grows out of the barrel of a gun'. She is formally committed to a radical revolutionary communism, not only for herself but as a prescription for the remedy of everybody's ills. She calls herself 'the storm centre of the world revolution'. All this combines to make her the supreme question-mark of our age. What is her future to be? If conflict with the Western world or with the Soviet Union is not inevitable, is it probable? Has the Western world a choice of policies towards China which could determine whether the outcome is peace or war?

The legacy of the past
As with Soviet Russia, past history colours present events in China and the attitude of the rulers of China to the world outside. All the features of present-day China, her self-chosen isolation, her instinctive assumptions of superiority over other nations, her aggressive gestures towards the Western great powers, have their roots in the long and often agonising experience of the Chinese people. For centuries, from the beginning of her history in 1500 BC, China dominated the vast area east of the Himalayas, regarding herself, and being regarded by others, as 'the Middle Kingdom', the very centre and source of civilisation. From the earliest times she undertook a kind of civilising mission among the more primitive people of Asia. Up to the fifteenth century, she had little or no contact with Europe and such impact as there was between the two was made, not by Europe on China, but by China on Europe. Reversing the situation we found in Imperial Russia, China at this time was technologically in advance of the Western world. She was the source of many of the basic inventions and discoveries which were later to become the foundations of knowledge in the world at large and of modern industrial development. Dr Joseph Needham in *Science and Civilisation in China* lists among processes first invented by the Chinese: an efficient harness for draught animals which was later to transform European agriculture; the technology of iron and steel; deep drilling for oil; gunpowder, paper, the mechanical clock and basic engineering devices such as the driving-belt. The pride of the Chinese in an ancient civilisation is well-founded and their contempt for what were regarded as the upstart civilisations of the West, is not difficult to understand.

All the greater, in consequence, were the effects of the humiliations imposed on China from the mid-nineteenth century onwards by the Western nations and Japan. Despite her early technological lead, China stood outside the scientific and industrial revolutions of the seventeenth and eighteenth centuries which turned the countries of Western Europe into powerful industrial and military states. Beginning with the Opium War of 1840, which was an attempt by Britain to maintain against Chinese wishes the profitable export of the drug to China, the Western governments using their superior material and military power, broke down the isolation of China and established a hold over her trade and commerce which was to last a hundred years. Chinese capitalists, who were created by foreign economic influence, fostered in turn a new class of absentee Chinese landlords who ruthlessly exploited the peasants. The inflow of foreign goods virtually destroyed native village industries. Under treaties imposed on successive emperors, the Western powers policed China, or parts of it, with their own military and naval forces, controlled Chinese customs services and set up foreign enclaves in and around the 'treaty' ports where jurisdiction was taken out of Chinese hands and placed in their own.

The Western presence brought, it is true, certain benefits to the Chinese though some of these were of doubtful value to say the least. Missionaries and teachers from Britain, the United States and some of the countries of Western Europe tried conscientiously to serve the spiritual and educational needs of the people. Western resources were lavishly used to build not only factories but hospitals, schools and universities. But, in general, the effect of foreign intervention was to reduce China to the status of a semi-colonial country. At best, the system was paternalistic and since it went along with economic exploitation and military control, it was bound to be resented and eventually rejected by a proud people with thousands of years of independence and civilisation behind them.

The fall of the Manchus
The turning-point in China's modern history came with the revolution of 1911 which led to the fall of the Manchus, the last of the great Imperial dynasties, and the founding of the Chinese Republic. Nearly forty years were to pass before

Left, Sun Yat-sen:
founder of modern
China; below, Chiang
Kai-shek: President of
Nationalist China and
ruler of Taiwan
(Formosa)

foreign intervention was finally ended and Chinese unity and independence secured, but the setting-up of the Republic under Sun Yat-sen, marked the beginning of the revolutionary changes in China which were to culminate in the communist take-over in 1949. Sun Yat-sen was the acknowledged founder of modern China and the inspirer of a doctrine and a programme for the Nationalists which was to serve Kuomintang (Nationalist) governments for the next two decades. He was appointed Provisional President of the new Republic in December, 1911. But he failed to gain effective authority over the Chinese armed forces and gave way to Yüan Shih-k'ai who became President. Sun regained power on the death of Yüan in 1916 but only on a precarious basis since by this time, China was in the grip of war-lords who split up the country and kept it in a state of perpetual conflict. Sun died in 1925, without ever becoming the effective ruler of the whole of China. One year earlier, he had taken a step which was to mark a portent for the future of his country. Despairing of effective support from the Western democracies for the new Republic, he came to an understanding with Soviet Russia and admitted the Chinese communists into his Nationalist Party —the Kuomintang. Sun's successor, Chiang K'ai-shek, who had no love for the communists, launched a campaign against them, driving them into the mountains of south-west China from which they ultimately emerged to seize the whole of China in 1949, and to drive Chiang and his Nationalist forces into the off-shore island of Formosa (Taiwan) where they remain today. The greatest and, so far, the last of China's open civil wars had begun.

Submission to Japan

We shall look, in a moment, at the significance of the communist triumph of 1949 and at the failures and successes of their revolution. But a word must first be said about the reaction of the foreign powers mainly interested in China to these events. Japan had inflicted a humiliating defeat on China in the war of 1894–95. Ten years later her victory over Russia, in the Russian-Japanese war of 1905, had strengthened her position in Asia and sharpened her rivalries with China.

In 1915, taking advantage of the weaknesses of China and the involvement of the Western great powers in the First World War, Japan forced upon China a series of harsh impositions known as the Twenty-One Demands which China was too weak to reject. In 1931 Japan, now in the grip of imperialist ambitions, seized the northern Chinese province of Manchuria with its vital mineral resources and set up the former boy Emperor of China (P'u Yi) as puppet ruler of 'Manchukuo'. Six years later Japan occupied most of the ports and cities of China, driving the Chinese Nationalist Government to Chungking which was to be the capital of the so-called Free China through the Second World War and the Japanese occupation. Chiang Kai-shek's sympathies had always been with the United States (American Methodists had earlier converted him to Christianity) and it was chiefly American power which sustained him in his resistance to the Japanese, secured Allied recognition of him as the acknowledged ruler of China when the war ended and supported him in his exile in Formosa, once the Chinese Communists had come to power on the mainland.

Mao Tse-tung, who was eventually to become the undisputed leader of China, held a military command in the early years of the Republic but in 1924 at the age of thirty-eight he went to Berlin to study and a year later joined the Communist Party. Three years later having returned to China, he began to organise a communist army in the south-west of China where later, in defiance of Chiang Kai-shek, the Chinese Soviet Republic was set up with Mao as Chairman and Chu Teh as the commander of its armies. Faced by pressure from the Nationalists, the communists embarked on the Long March of the autumn of 1934 which, in a trek of six thousand miles, brought them to new headquarters at Yenan in a bend of the Yellow River, in the north-western province of Shensi.

The Communist Revolution

This famous march which is regarded as one of the great dramatic events of history, had a toughening effect on the communist forces and prepared them for the successful final struggle against the Nationalists. Less than ten thousand survived the march but these were to form the nucleus of the communist armies which fifteen years later, in January 1949, were to make a triumphal entry into Peking when Chiang and his Nationalist followers fled to Formosa (Taiwan) and the People's Republic of China, to use the official title, came into being. Thanks to the good behaviour of the soldiers, the communist armies were well received by the Chinese masses as they made their victorious journey to the capital. But once in power in Peking, the new rulers began ruthlessly to establish their revolution. In the first three years their determination to remove any vestiges of opposition led not only to the dispossession of the former landlords but to the violent liquidation of two to three million Chinese who were judged to be hostile to the revolution or likely to obstruct its aims.

The undoubted social achievements of the revolution after that period, were gained at the price of a ruthlessly-imposed ideological and political conformity and the virtual militarisation of the whole country—'the substitution', to quote a telling phrase of an experienced French observer, Robert Guillain, 'of mental poverty for material poverty, the death of the cultivation of the mind'. The gains were made, that is to say, at the price of personal and political freedoms which we in the West would regard, or profess to regard as precious, though they were freedoms, it must be admitted, which only a minority of Chinese had enjoyed in the past. Nevertheless the social gains of the revolution, at least in the early stages, were real enough. China was at peace internally for the first time in generations; there was no open civil war; the fighting war lords had vanished. Administration under the communists was (for China) remarkably honest; corruption was eliminated and so were, to quote Guillain again, 'the smells, the squalor, the rags, the beggars and the dirt'—many of the symbols, in fact, of the old China. Living conditions were still poor by Western standards but economic conditions for the masses had visibly improved and some stability of prices had been achieved. Most important of all was the fact that, perhaps as never before, the great majority of the Chinese felt it to be their country; they felt it to be their government, too, not only in name but in fact.

Popular education—reading the news

The Sino-Soviet quarrel

In the 1960s, two events—the quarrel with Soviet Russia and the Cultural Revolution within China itself—tended to slow down the steady, if gradual, progress of the new China. From the beginning, the Russians had given to the new China, not only the moral and ideological support which one communist government might be expected to give to another, but also economic and financial aid in the development of the country. Thousands of Soviet technicians were sent to China to assist in the modernisation programme of the Chinese government, to plan and to build the dams, the factories and the power stations which were necessary to the country's economic growth. In August 1957, following a series of differences which had begun to show themselves after the death of Stalin and the new directions taken by Soviet policy, the 12,000 Soviet technicians were abruptly withdrawn, together with the plans to which they were working. The era of close economic cooperation was drawing to an end; the gulf between the two communist giants began to widen and by the later sixties, the breach was complete. China rejected Soviet leadership of the communist bloc and excluded herself from international communist conferences and consultations. She began a violent propaganda campaign against the Soviet leaders, charging them with a reversion to capitalism and a betrayal of the Marxist-Leninist revolution of which henceforth China was to become, in its own eyes, the only true and faithful defender.

The causes of this rift in the camp of Socialism were varied and complicated. It was not so much the ends of policy that were in dispute; both Soviet Russia and China remained and remain formally committed to the building of communism. The differences related to the methods to be used in the building of communism and above all to the timing and the speed with which they could be fulfilled. Where relations with the developing world of Asia, Africa and Latin America were concerned, the issue was how best to encourage revolutionary situations likely to serve ultimate communist aims in these areas. But the dispute was also over the leadership of the communist bloc itself. Were the smaller communist countries and parties to look for inspiration and guidance to Moscow or Peking? Above all, the dispute was about the global strategy of communism and its attitude to the great powers of the West. The Russians, as we have seen, were in favour on the whole of improving or at least stabilising their relations with the United States and the West generally, if only because of the risks of mutual involvement in nuclear war. This rewriting of Lenin's and Stalin's teaching on war and peace and the correct attitude for communists to adopt to 'capitalist-imperialists' was dangerous heresy in the view of the Chinese leaders and totally unacceptable to them. They were too intelligent not to see that if nuclear war happened, immense destruction would fall on all the countries involved but they persuaded themselves that, even so, a sizeable remnant of the Chinese people would survive and, to quote a Chinese army journal, 'would build for themselves a beautiful future on the debris of a dead imperialism.' Therefore, said the Chinese, there was a case not for relaxing the communist attitude to the imperialist world but for making it even more militant.

Perhaps at bottom, these differences between the Soviet Russia and China can be taken to reflect the relative ages of the two communist revolutions. After nearly fifty years the Russians needed a breathing-space, a period of peace, to

The Cultural Revolution: demonstration in the Tien an Men Square, Peking

consolidate the gains of their revolution of 1917 and to extend
the practical benefits of their economic growth to the mass of
the people. The Chinese Revolution is still only twenty years
old. China, despite her achievement of a nuclear capacity,
is still only at the outset of the economic development
necessary to turn her into a modern industrial state. Her
leaders know that they must maintain revolutionary fervour
if they are to get from the Chinese people the sacrifices which
economic modernisation demands. They know that their hold
on the Chinese masses depends on their convincing them,
despite any evidence to the contrary, that they are engaged in a
ruthless struggle against forces determined to destroy them.
The chief enemy, which conveniently is 'American imperialism', has to be depicted, therefore, much bigger than
life-size; the myth of a hostile imperialism from which China
must be protected, has to be maintained.

The Cultural Revolution
All these trends, including the quarrel with the Soviet
Union, were strengthened by the Great Proletarian Cultural
Revolution which Mao Tse-tung and his closest colleagues
unleashed in the spring of 1966. The declared purpose of the
Cultural Revolution was to revive and intensify the original
revolutionary spirit—'to revolutionise peoples' ideology', as a

statement of August, 1966 put it, 'and as a consequence to achieve greater, faster, better and more economical results in all fields of work.' But the campaign was also designed to confirm Mao and his friends as the undisputed leaders of China and to confound those in the leadership, including the then President of China, Liu Shao-chi, who questioned Mao's policies and wanted a more flexible and modern approach to the solving of China's social and economic problems. In June 1966, at Mao's insistence the schools and universities were closed and scholars and students throughout the country were encouraged, first to reform the old educational system—a task they achieved by abusing their teachers and destroying their textbooks—so as to build a new one conforming to Maoist ideals and then to reform the whole Chinese society and purge it of allegedly anti-communist and anti-revolutionary ideas. The Red Guard movement, as it came to be known, sprang into being in August 1966 in a mass meeting in Peking attended by a million school-children and students. The assembled Chinese youth were urged by Lin Piao, now Mao's closest comrade-in-arms, to destroy what little remained of traditional Chinese society and all bourgeois, capitalist and revisionist ideas. The Red Guards took to the streets, destroyed so-called bourgeois property, violently used any who dared to oppose them and inflicted humiliation and maltreatment on thousands who were said to belong to the old bourgeoisie. Later they shifted their attack to alleged opponents of Mao in the Communist Party and the Government, dragging local leaders and civil servants into the streets where they were publicly humiliated. Life in China became one continuous demonstration; all education was suspended and industrial production fell, by about 15% in 1967.

Mao and his colleagues, it soon became clear, had bitten off more than they could chew. The Red Guards were eventually urged to return to their schools and to place themselves under discipline, an instruction that was only fulfilled the better part of a year later when the Chinese army, or The Peoples' Liberation Army as it is called, was brought in to compel the Red Guards to return to their studies and to restore the authority of the local officials of the Communist Party. Even

Mao Tse-tung briefs his heir apparent : army leader, Lin Piao

so, the summer of 1967 saw a steadily increasing disorder throughout China, including armed clashes between Red Guards and workers. The Peoples' Liberation Army intervened again, this time on its own initiative, not to involve itself as earlier, in the local political struggles between Mao's supporters and opponents, but to forestall anarchy and re-establish at least a degree of law and order. Authority was restored to local Party officials who had been discredited and displaced and the students were told to return to their desks. An edict of August, 1968 required the students to integrate themselves with the new 'worker-peasant-soldier Mao's thought-propaganda teams'. The long task began of making up the leeway in production that had been lost in two years of revolutionary upheaval.

The challenge of China
The end of the Great Proletarian Cultural Revolution saw the instruments of power still in the hands of Mao Tse-tung and his friends. Nevertheless, the struggle between the ideologues—those who want to put revolutionary zeal and purpose first—and the technocrats who want to see China take her place rapidly as a modern State in a modern world, remains

the vital issue facing China today. Whatever the outcome of
this struggle, there is little doubt that China will continue to
challenge and perplex the established countries of the West
and remain the focus of attraction for revolutionary movements especially in the under-privileged areas of the world.
The Chinese communists have had only limited success in
penetrating the new Africa with their influence because of the
determination of most of the African states not to compromise
their new-found independence and to take a neutral attitude
towards the great powers of East or West. But China's
'communism of the poor', as Robert Guillain described it, is
still likely to have more appeal for the deprived peoples
whether in Africa, Asia or elsewhere, than the Soviet Union's
'communism of the rich', with its emphasis on space research,
advanced techniques in all fields and almost American
standards of life. China's approach to nuclear power status
does not affect this basic fact. She could still offer to the poor
world a way to communism more suited to its needs.

Neither past history nor present trends in China suggest
that her rulers are likely to undertake any deliberate and direct
act of aggression against their Asian neighbours or the West,
though China's political influence in Asia is likely to grow,
especially in those countries where there are large numbers of
people of Chinese racial origin. In time, population pressures
within China might force her to a policy of expansion beyond
her present frontiers and the four thousand mile land frontier
between her and the U.S.S.R. could become the 'flash-point'
of an open conflict. (There was sporadic fighting at its
southern end during 1969.) But China's annexation of Tibet,
and her raids in 1961 into the frontier areas which separate
her from India, are evidence not so much of a deliberate
policy of expansion, as of a determination to reverse the
humiliations imposed upon her by the Western powers in the
days of her weakness and to restore the historic boundaries of
the ancient China.

China and the West
China's future role in world affairs and her relations with
the established countries of the West, may be influenced to

some degree by the attitudes these countries themselves adopt towards China. Great Britain, believing that the communist regime had come to stay and anxious to maintain and develop economic and trading relations with the new China, gave diplomatic recognition to the People's Republic soon after it came into being in 1949. The United States, seeing a united and militantly communist China as a possible threat to its security in the Pacific, and determined to resist the spread of communism anywhere in the world, continued to support General Chiang Kai-shek and his Nationalist forces in Formosa (Taiwan) and put itself at the head of those who were determined not to give any aid or comfort, diplomatic or other, to the new Chinese rulers. In due course, the American Seventh Fleet was stationed between Formosa and the Chinese mainland where it still remains; in principle to prevent a resumption of the Chinese civil war but effectively to protect the Chinese Nationalists on Formosa from any attack from the communist side. In the United Nations, the United States maintained uncompromising opposition to the admission of the Chinese communist regime to the world organisation, saying that communist China had been branded an aggressor in Korea by a resolution of the General Assembly, that its presence in the United Nations would not be conducive to world peace and security and that, in any case, the Nationalists on Formosa were still the legitimate government of China and, as such, entitled to represent China within the organisation. Since 1950, by decree of the United States government, no American has been allowed to engage in trade with China.

The ending of the war in Vietnam may, in time, moderate the hostile attitudes of Peking and Washington to each other and make possible some compromise solution of the problem of China's representation in the United Nations. One suggestion, so far rejected by both the United States and the People's Republic, would give the People's Republic the seat and the powers of *China* within the world organisation (including its place in the Security Council) and give Formosa separate representation as *Formosa* and as an independent State. Formosa is today a territory as large and as economically self-supporting as many a State already in independent membership of the United Nations. The entry of the Chinese communists into the organisation, assuming that when the time came they would wish to enter, would not automatically solve all the problems of China's relations with the outside world nor is it likely, in the short run, to make the atmosphere in the United Nations more harmonious or productive. But it would make possible China's participation in efforts to achieve world disarmament and mark the beginning of a movement to break down the dangerous isolation of China and bring her into a more normal relationship with the rest of the world. 'The historical drama of China's adjustment to the world', Richard Harris has said, 'is a compelling one. The world's realisation of what this adjustment means will not be achieved without, in turn, the world adjusting itself to China.' China will, before long, have the capacity to deliver nuclear weapons across the earth. Her population which was estimated to stand at 720 million in mid-1967, is increasing by 1·4%, that is by ten millions a year. Within twenty years, it is estimated, one in every three human beings alive will be Chinese. There can be no settled peace in the world until China has 'joined the human race' and taken her place in the cooperative enterprises which the survival of humanity demands.

TOPICS FOR DISCUSSION

- What kind of country and people do you think of when China is mentioned today?

- Why were a relatively small band of Chinese Communists able to gain control of six hundred million Chinese? How important for the world at large are the revolutionary changes they are carrying through in China?

- What steps could be taken by the western world to encourage China to come out of its present isolation and take an active and peaceful part in world affairs?

7

Plans for peace

Dr James Shotwell, a leading American internationalist once pointed out that movements to rid the world of war never became really influential in the policies and actions of nations until, beginning in 1914, war changed its nature under the impact of science and began to threaten the very future of mankind. 'Older than history, with roots in the savage world', as he put it, 'war remained for centuries the test of sovereignty and of power among nations—even those which took pride in being civilised.' It is true that attempts were made from the seventeenth century onwards to make rules for the conduct of warfare in the hope of limiting its scope and reducing its horrors. But war remained the final argument in disputes between states. Despite humanitarian movements protesting fitfully against war, all governments resorted to war, whenever 'the national interest' or the declared objectives of the state seemed to demand it, a practice they have still not entirely abandoned.

Even so, throughout the centuries men have had visions of a world at peace and have devised plans and institutions which were to outlaw war and make possible the peaceful settlement of the differences that must occur between rulers and states. Some of these designs remained visionary; they never got off the drawing-board, as it were. Others have taken practical shape in organisations which though frequently ineffective, nevertheless achieved some results and marked a stage in the gradual progress towards world order. The ancient Greeks made some of the first exercises in the cooperation of sovereign bodies or groups for common ends. Members of their Amphictionic League undertook not to destroy or cut off running water from any city belonging to the League. All the city-states of the Peloponnese, with the exception of Argos and Achaea, were joined in a loose confederacy called the Peloponnesian League whose members undertook to supply military contingents for common defence. The League met in Sparta and each member sent representatives. Later, for a period of five hundred years, peace was maintained in Europe, parts of Asia and North Africa under institutions established by the Romans and the systems of taxation and law they imposed on the then civilised world. This was the *Pax Romana*, the peace kept by the unchallenged might of Rome, which was run on the principle of toleration and order for those who did not oppose Roman authority and ruthless severity against those who did. In the Middle Ages, the Holy Roman Empire which had succeeded to the Western half of the secular Roman Empire and was based on the idea of the solidarity of Christendom, held together in an uneasy and often quarrelsome alliance, Germany, Austria, Italy, France, Denmark, Poland and other states. Under the authority of the Pope and the Emperor there was imposed a kind of international law and rules of conduct which held sway over large areas of Central and Western Europe. In the eighteenth and nineteenth centuries the *Pax Britannica*—the system of imperial rule based largely on the overwhelming naval power of Britain—kept the peace over wide areas of Asia, Africa and the Southern seas and the trade routes of the world.

The century of alliances

Meanwhile in 1815, the Congress of Vienna which followed the Napoleonic Wars, marked the beginning of the alliances between states and their rulers based on the principle of the balance of power, which in their various combinations dominated the affairs of Europe until 1914. In the Holy Alliance sponsored by the then Tsar Alexander in 1815, Russia, Austria and Prussia pledged themselves to apply justice, Christian charity and peace to international relations. Joined by England to make the Quadruple Alliance, they pledged themselves not only to exclude Napoleon's heirs from the throne of France but to keep inviolate the political and territorial arrangements of the Congress of Vienna. Joined later by France, the nations of the Quadruple Alliance pledged themselves in the so-called Concert of Europe, to maintain peace and the existing order in the European

After Napoleon : the Congress of Vienna shapes the future.

continent, a kind of mutual insurance for the monarchies of Europe to preserve their dynasties. For a time they not only preserved their dynasties but peace as well; for more than fifty years after 1815, there was no large-scale European war.

The first blue-prints

All these arrangements were based on the overwhelming power of a single state, as in the *Pax Romana* or the *Pax Britannica*, or on alliances between states, which served on occasions to maintain peace but could be used and were used as instruments of war, if some challenge to the alliance arose from outside. A peace so organised was bound to be uncertain and dependent in the last resort on the peaceful intentions of individual states and their rulers. Inevitably, therefore, thinkers and philosophers throughout the centuries have set themselves to prepare schemes under which the sovereignty of individual states would be transcended and some measure of international authority imposed on the separate nations. As early as 1306, Pierre Dubois, a French jurist and politician, was proposing the formation of a General Council representing all Christian states under the Presidency of the Pope, with its policing power to be supplied by France. The member-nations were to submit their differences to a tribunal for arbitration and those who were dissatisfied with its rulings could appeal to the Pope himself. Something akin to the sanctions system—the system of enforcing international decisions by military or economic pressures—as we know it today, was seen in the provision whereby those who refused to submit their disputes to arbitration or to abide by their under-takings, could be excommunicated by the Pope. Four years later, Dante in his *De Monarchia* suggested a kind of universal federation whose peace would be guaranteed by one ruler.

Three hundred years later in 1623, Emeric Cruce, a French monk, devised (in *The new Cyneas*) a plan which is sometimes regarded as the original blueprint for the system of interna-tional organisation that we have today. Cruce suggested the formation of a permanent Council of Ambassadors to meet in Venice. The Council would settle differences between Princes by majority vote and condemn to disgrace those who rejected its decisions. If necessary, the Council would be defended by the joint military power of the Princes through a kind of universal police 'useful equally to all nations and acceptable to those which have some light of reason and sentiment of humanity'. The Council was to exercise legis-lative power in order 'to meet discontents half way and appease them by gentle means if it could be done or in the case of necessity, by force.' The all-embracing membership was to include 'the Pope, the Emperor of the Turks, the Jews, the Kings of Persia and China, the Grand Duke of Muscovy and Monarchs from India and Africa'. Three centuries were to elapse before Cruce's design was to become reality but all the major principles embodied in the League of Nations in 1919 and later in the United Nations, were to be found in his plan. He can be regarded in a real sense, as original inspirer of both organisations.

The peace of Europe

Seventy years later as the seventeenth century was drawing to a close, William Penn, the English Quaker, who later founded Pennsylvania, published his essay *Towards the Present and Future Peace of Europe*. 'Peace', he wrote, 'is the fruit of justice and justice is the fruit of government designed by men of peace.' His was the concept, therefore, of a European Diet or Parliament to which sovereign princes would send their deputies and to which all disputes not settled by direct negotiation were to be referred for decision. Since in all such plans the basis of representation is a crucial question, it is noteworthy that Penn saw the need to vary the representation of the state-members of his proposed Diet according to such factors as their military power, their revenues, their exports and imports. Germany for example was to have twelve deputies; England only six. Again the principle of the enforcement of decisions found a place; member-states were to combine their military strengths to compel a state to submit its disputes or complaints to the Diet and to accept its decisions. Among the benefits and the savings to be derived from his plan, the thrifty Quaker noted 'the great expense that frequent and splendid Embassies require and all their appendages of spies and intelligence'.

During the eighteenth century two philosophic thinkers—one French, one English—produced designs for peace notable in both cases for their emphasis on the need to resolve disputes not by war, but by resort to arbitration and third-party judgment. The French Abbé de Saint-Pierre in his minutely-detailed *Project to bring Perpetual Peace to Europe* published in 1713, urged the twenty-four states of Christian Europe to form a Grand Alliance or European Union controlled by a Senate of Peace which was to be permanently in session. This Senate of Peace was to be stationed in Utrecht; its President was to change weekly and to have the title of The Prince of Peace. Disputes were to be referred to Mediating Commissioners appointed by the Senate and if they failed to settle it, the matter was to be referred to the compulsory arbitration of the Senate itself. Again the combined armies of the Alliance were to discipline any state refusing to abide by the collective decision of the Senate, or engaging in preparations for war.

Towards the end of the same century in 1789, on the eve of the Napoleonic wars, Jeremy Bentham produced a *Plan for a Universal and Perpetual Peace* which envisaged an International Court and an International Legislature, both having power to enforce their decisions and awards. But Bentham's plan had two novel features. More than a hundred and fifty years before the great powers gave independence to their dependent territories, Bentham urged France and Britain to free their colonies and, in a new emphasis in plans of this nature, he urged them to reduce their armed forces to an agreed level. Six years later in 1795, the German philosopher Kant, in his plan named *Perpetual Peace*, was proposing a Confederation of Nations and the gradual abolition of national armed forces. Greatly ahead of his time, he advocated also a world citizenship and freedom of movement based on a universal law of hospitality.

One other name, that of the Austrian Baroness Bertha von Suttner, deserves an honourable mention among the pioneers of peace. The Baroness produced no plans or blueprints but she wrote, towards the end of the nineteenth century, a book *Lay Down Your Arms*, which effectively dramatised the need for arbitration, disarmament and world organisation. Moreover, she was the true inspirer of the unofficial and international peace movement which began to develop at that time, the forerunner of the numerous peace groups and organisations of today.

The Hague Conferences

None of the dreams or the plans of these writers and philosophers became realities in their time but most, if not all of them, had some influence on the systems of international organisation which were later to be established. The Abbé de Saint-Pierre and Jeremy Bentham in particular, with their emphasis on the settlement of international disputes by arbitration, paved the way for the conferences held at The Hague in Holland, which marked the beginning of the modern effort to build institutional defences against war. At the first Hague Peace Conference, summoned in 1899 on the initiative of Tsar Nicholas the Second of Russia, the representatives of twenty-six nations established Commissions on Armaments and Weapons and on the Usages of War and Arbitration.

Eight years later, a second Hague Conference, proposed this time by President Theodore Roosevelt of the United States, was attended by forty-four nations. Failing to recognise that the Industrial Revolution which had swept over Europe was transforming not only the techniques of peace but also the techniques of war, the statesmen at The Hague concentrated on attempts to limit and humanise war by regulating the practices of war and by defining the rights and duties of neutrals. But they also agreed on a Convention for the Pacific Settlement of International Disputes in which mediation and arbitration were recommended as methods of settling differences and of preventing war. Out of the first Hague meeting came the Permanent Court of Arbitration which was later to become first the Permanent Court of International Justice of the League of Nations and then the International Court of Justice, now known as the World Court, of the United Nations.

The League of Nations
It may seem a far cry from the hopes and visions of the seventeenth-century Frenchman, Emeric Cruce to the League of Nations of 1920 but, as we have seen, it was in the League organisation that his ideas, and later the ideas of his fellow-philosophers, first took practical and recognisable shape. The League was born in the agony and destruction of the First World War and in the minds of progressive statesmen such as President Wilson of the United States, Lord Robert Cecil of Great Britain and General Smuts of South Africa, who worked out their schemes while the war was still raging. Its establishment was a major landmark in the development of international machinery for the prevention of war and the promotion of economic cooperation across frontiers.

Failure and achievement
In the event, the League failed in its central task, the prevention of war. But, even on the political side, it helped to settle disputes—over Memel, over the Aaland Islands, over Upper Silesia, between Greece and Bulgaria, between Poland and Lithuania to mention no others—all of which involved areas which might have become battlefields. Achievements

were registered in other fields also and foundations laid on which eventually the successor-organisation, the United Nations could be more easily and more surely built. Under the League's Mandates System, as we noted in Chapter Four, the victorious powers of the First World War made themselves accountable to the international authority for their administration of the colonial territories they had taken over from the defeated enemies—Germany and Turkey—pending the readiness of these territories to govern themselves. Through its Committee on Intellectual Cooperation, the League also laid foundations for the world-wide cooperation in the fields of education, culture and science which was later to be developed in the United Nations Educational, Scientific and Cultural Organisation. It was the League, moreover, which began the cooperative international effort to deal with economic and social problems which was later to become a central feature of the United Nations.

The League of Nations had come into being on the wave of hope and idealism which followed the ending of the greatest war in history. At its inception, Lord Curzon, speaking in the House of Lords and reflecting the mood of the times, quoted from the chorus from Shelley's *Hellas*, the confident words: 'The world's great age begins anew, the golden years return.' In reality, from the outset, the League's hopes of success were small. The American Congress, reflecting the still powerful isolationism of the United States, rejected the Treaty of Versailles together with their own President Wilson's proposals for a League of Nations, and remained outside the League to the end. The new and revolutionary Russia was not admitted till 1934 when Germany and Japan had already fallen into the grip of strongly aggressive forces and were about to leave. The failure of the great powers within the League to respond firmly to the moral and political challenges of Japan's invasion of Manchuria in 1931 and Italy's invasion of Abyssinia in 1935, proved to be the prelude to the Second World War and the final breakdown of the League itself.

The end of the League

The failure of the United States to join the League of Nations marked a weakness in the organisation which it never fully overcame. More fundamentally still, the League suffered from its built-in association with the punitive Treaty of Versailles and, subsequently, from the unreadiness of the member-states who were great powers, to support the League in taking the steps that were necessary to forestall or stop aggression. The rise and fall of the League emphasises, in fact, the vital truth which applies equally, as we shall see, to the United Nations that however excellent and necessary may be the social and humanitarian work of international organisations such as the League, nothing that is lasting can be achieved even in these fields, unless war itself can be prevented and peace maintained. When the Second World War broke out the League inevitably foundered, 'swept away' in the phrase of Paul Henri Spaak, the Belgian statesman, 'by the force of the gale'. Spaak went on to say: 'However, a great dream must eventually recur. Great practical and social experiments will always be repeated if the idea on which they are based is sound. In the long run hope always prevails over discouragement.' The dream was to recur, the hope was to be renewed, if in a rather more sober mood, in the United Nations.

TOPICS FOR DISCUSSION

- Can we have peace without the institutions of peace—the international organisations which exist to provide security for all peoples and to promote international action for their common welfare?

- Was the failure of the League of Nations due to weaknesses in its structure or to other factors and circumstances?

8

The United Nations

The statesmen who in the midst of the Second World War began to plan the organisation known as the United Nations, chose to create a new structure rather than build on the ruins of the old. They hoped, in this way, to spare the new organisation the disrepute it might earn if it was associated in the public mind with a League of Nations which had to all intents and purposes collapsed at the onset of war. In formal terms, then, the United Nations was a new body with some not unimportant differences in its make-up from the old League. Nevertheless in broad outline the two organisations had a common shape as well as a common purpose. The United Nations can be seen, therefore, as the end-product to date of the process we have examined in the previous chapter. It can be seen as the latest and most ambitious of the steps, taken or proposed by states and statesmen over the centuries, to organise a world freed from war.

In a real sense, then, the origins of the United Nations lie deep in history. But the impulses which brought it into being in the closing stages of the Second World War, came directly from the war itself and the catastrophic experiences the war had brought to governments and peoples alike. Vast resources of men and material had been thrown into the struggle and immense losses had been sustained by all the combatants. The world lay shocked and bleeding and much of it was literally in ruins. There were gigantic tasks of reconstruction to be undertaken. Above all, as we have seen, the explosion in the final days of the war, of the first atomic bombs over Japan, opened up a future prospect of violence and destruction, of new and terrifying dimensions. Small wonder that the leaders of the nations saw it as a sacred duty 'to save', as the Charter of the United Nations later expressed it, 'succeeding generations from the scourge of war', and to establish whatever system of international cooperation might best achieve this end.

Evening on the East River : the United Nations building

In one respect, the founders of the United Nations had an advantage over their predecessors of 1919. In skeleton form, much of the organisation they needed for the purposes of reconstruction lay ready to hand in the machinery they had created for the more effective conduct of the war. A vast system of mutual aid had been created to ensure the defeat of Hitlerism. Its immediate goal was military victory, but this could not be achieved by military means alone. The economic and social needs of the allied peoples had to be met and their morale maintained. Beyond this, the peace aims of the western allies—the ends for which they claimed to be fighting —had to be made convincing in visible steps to improve the lot of their own peoples, even while the fighting continued.

From war to peace

So there was available, as the war closed, a structure of inter-allied organisation which with relatively little difficulty could be adapted to meet post-war needs and to provide a continuing means of cooperation between the nations. A few examples can be given of this adaptation of war-time machinery to the needs and institutions of peace. The discussions on the financial problems of the allies, held at Bretton Woods in the United States in 1944, led to the setting-up of the International Bank for Reconstruction and Development and its stable companion, the International Monetary Fund. A conference on the food needs of the allied peoples in war-time, held also in the United States and as early as 1943, prepared the way for the World Food and Agriculture Organisation, now commonly known as F.A.O. A Council of the Ministers of Education of the allied countries, held in London in the dark days of 1942, three years before the war ended, laid the foundations of the international organisation now known conveniently as UNESCO.

Most of these functional organisations were to become the so-called specialised agencies of the United Nations and to their role and significance today, we turn in the next chapter. Meanwhile the centre-piece of all this international organisation, the United Nations itself, had been taking shape gradually in a series of declarations in which the western allies, either alone or in company with the Soviet Union, had from time to time defined the kind of peace they hoped to establish after the war. An Inter-Allied Declaration, signed in London in June, 1941 by representatives of the governments of the British Commonwealth (Canada, S. Africa, New Zealand and Australia) and of the exiled European governments temporarily housed in Britain (Norway, Denmark, Belgium, Holland and Poland) and by General de Gaulle representing Free France, defined 'as the only true basis of enduring peace the willing cooperation of free peoples in a world, in which relieved of the menace of aggression, all may enjoy economic and social security'. Two months later, meeting on a warship in mid-Atlantic, President Roosevelt of the United States and Prime Minister Churchill of Great Britain, issued the celebrated Atlantic Charter in which they expressed their hope, 'once the Nazi tyranny had been destroyed to see established a peace which will afford to all nations the means of dwelling in safety within their own boundaries and which will afford assurance that all the men in all the lands may live out their lives in freedom from fear and want'. In January 1942, in a Declaration of Washington, in which the phrase 'United Nations' was formally used for the first time, the twenty-six allied nations reaffirmed their determination to pursue the war to final victory and confirmed their support for the principles of the Atlantic Charter. In October 1943, the representatives of the United States, the Soviet Union, Britain and China, in a Declaration on General Security made in Moscow,

> recognised the necessity to establish at the earliest practicable date, a general international organisation based on the principle of the sovereign equality of all peace-loving states and open to membership by all such states, large and small, for the maintenance of peace and international security.

The first designs

These, then, were the declarations of intent which foreshadowed and fostered the idea of a United Nations organisation. The first blue-print for the organisation itself emerged from a conference held at Dumbarton Oaks in Washington

Above, Britain signs the United Nations Charter, June 1945; below, Churchill, Roosevelt and Stalin at Yalta

between August and October, 1944 and was further considered by Roosevelt, Churchill and Stalin at their meeting at Yalta in the Crimea in February, 1945. It was at Yalta, too, that the date was set for the formal inauguration of the United Nations at a conference to be convened at San Francisco in April of the same year. Before the end of June, the fifty nations assembled at San Francisco had agreed unanimously on the terms of the United Nations Charter and the terms of the Statute of the new International Court of Justice. On October 24th 1945, only two months after the war in Asia had ended, Charter and Statute came into force and the United Nations was a reality. Six grim years had passed since the virtual collapse of the old League. A new chapter had opened in the story of men's effort to organise a world at peace.

For the statesmen of the time, the central purpose of this United Nations which they rightly saw as the major positive outcome of the war, was to ensure that such a conflict and the events that had given rise to it, would not happen again. This purpose was set out in eloquent words in the Preamble to the Charter signed at San Francisco, which expressed the determination of 'we, the peoples of the United Nations', not only, in the words already quoted, 'to save succeeding generations from the scourge of war . . .' but also to 'reaffirm faith in fundamental human rights . . . to establish conditions under which justice and respect for the obligations arising from treaties and other sources of international law can be maintained, and to promote social progress and better standards of life in larger freedom'. With these ends in view, the founding-members of the United Nations pledged themselves to 'live together in peace as good neighbours', 'to unite their strength to maintain peace and security', 'to ensure that armed force would not be used except in the common interest' and 'to promote the economic and social advancement of all peoples.'

Machinery and method
We shall consider, presently, how far these pledges solemnly made at San Francisco in 1945, have been honoured in the ensuing years, and ask ourselves how much or how little

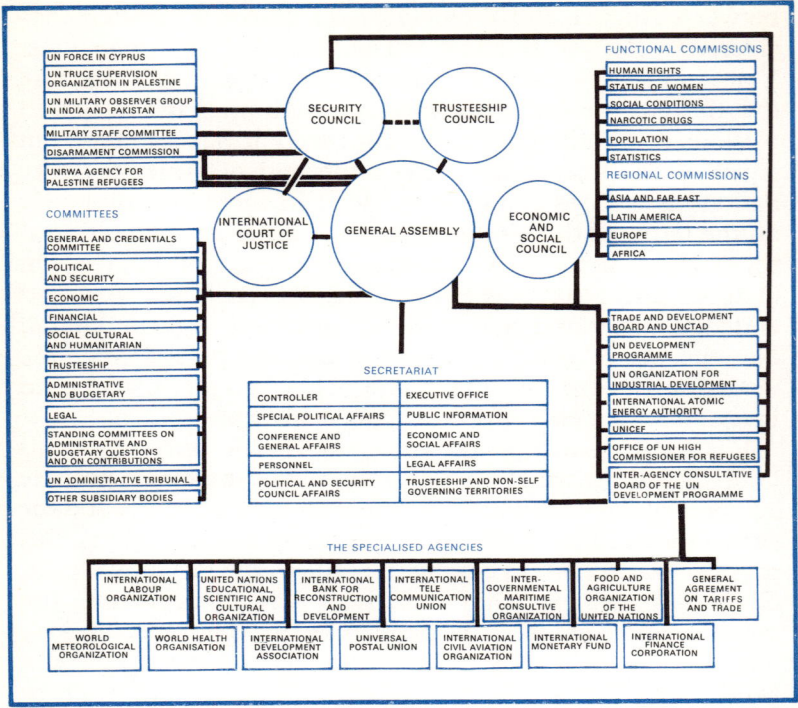

The structure of the United Nations

progress has been made in realising the objectives set out in the Charter. But first a word about the basic features of the United Nations and the machinery and methods it uses to carry out its work. The United Nations, as its name implies, is an organisation of states whose representation within the organisation is through their governments. The original fifty-one member-states were those countries which had cooperated in the war against Hitler and shared in the founding conference at San Francisco. By later additions, the number of member-states has now grown to one hundred and twenty-six, an increase which, as we shall see, has significantly changed the composition of the original United Nations and brought its own special problems, both organisational and political. The practice is for each member-state to maintain a

The Security Council debates Czechoslovakia, August 1968

permanent mission as it is called, at the headquarters of the organisation in New York. The former headquarters of the League of Nations in Geneva, have become the European office of the United Nations and the venue of many of its meetings. There are five official languages of the United Nations: Chinese, English, French, Russian and Spanish and in the General Assembly and its Committees, speeches are translated simultaneously into each of these tongues.

The United Nations carries out its tasks through six principal organs whose names broadly indicate what they do. They are the General Assembly, the Security Council, the Economic and Social Council, the Trusteeship Council, the International Court of Justice and, last but not least, the Secretariat. The General Assembly, to which each member-state, whether it is the tiny Nauru with 4,000 people or India with 500 million is entitled to send a delegation of equal size, is the major representative organ of the United Nations. Though it can be called specially in certain circumstances, its regular meeting is held each autumn, usually in New York. In the general debate on these occasions, the Foreign Ministers of the constituent states take a look at the world as it is and at the tasks facing the United Nations itself. The Assembly also receives reports from the more specialised bodies within the United Nations system and, later in its session, votes upon resolutions received from the seven main Committees to which its detailed work has been delegated. The Assembly can, in fact, consider any problem affecting international peace and security, unless the matter is actually being discussed by the Security Council, and it can make recommendations to member governments as to the actions they should take. The Assembly is not in any strict or constitutional sense, a world parliament with power to impose its decisions on member-states or their peoples. But it can properly be described as a world forum, though not yet a fully universal forum, in which from time to time, at least something like a world judgment and a world conscience can be expressed.

An inner group

The Security Council, which broadly corresponds to the Council of the old League of Nations, is an inner group of the United Nations with a limited membership dominated largely by the so-called great powers: France, the Soviet Union, the United States and Great Britain. These countries, together with China, have permanent seats on the Council and can each veto any decision the Council may desire to take. There are now ten (originally the number was six) non-permanent members of the Council who are elected by the General Assembly for a two-year period of membership and are usually chosen to ensure a balanced representation of the chief geographical areas of the world.

In theory at least, the Security Council is the seat of real power in the United Nations, not only because the big powers have a special standing within the Council through the veto but because under the Charter, the Council was given primary responsibility for the organisation of peace and security in the stricter meaning of these terms. It is for this body to decide whether a given situation is a threat to peace or whether an act of aggression against a member-state has taken place, and to make recommendations as to the action to be taken. It can call upon member-states to apply economic penalties or other measures short of war to prevent or stop aggression and it can, if it likes, make the requests mandatory—that is binding on the member-states. It can, in principle, take military action against a declared aggressor though, except in one unusual situation to which we shall refer, it has not done so to date. Among its other functions, the Security Council deals with the admission of new members of the United Nations, the appointment of the Secretary-General and the election of the judges of the International Court of Justice.

The welfare purpose

The Economic and Social Council now has a membership of twenty-three states, a portion of the membership being elected each year for a three-year period. This Council, which is responsible under the authority of the General Assembly for the economic and social activities of the United Nations, is the apex, as it were, of a whole pyramid of organisations, some of which we describe in Chapter Nine, whose task is the promotion of the well-being of the peoples of the world through trade and development, technical assistance, health, education, food and nutritional standards, atomic energy, conditions of labour, child welfare and so on. The Council itself holds an annual conference, usually in Geneva, but meetings of its numerous subsidiary bodies, agencies and committees are taking place constantly all over the world.

The Trusteeship Council of the United Nations was originally established to receive and examine reports on their stewardship from various governments and authorities which, under the so-called Trusteeship system of the United Nations, were regarded as trustees for territories not yet ready for independence or self-government. These territories included areas taken from the defeated enemy at the close of the First World War and administered under the Mandates system of the League of Nations (which had a similar purpose), as well as territories voluntarily brought within the scope of the Trustee-ship system by their administering governments. The work of

The World Court in session at The Hague

the Trusteeship Council has steadily diminished as former colonial territories have attained independence and membership in their own right in the United Nations.

The 'World Court'

The International Court of Justice is the successor to the Permanent Court of International Justice of the former League. It is the chief judicial organ of the United Nations and operates under its own Statute which forms an integral part of the Charter. All members of the United Nations are parties to the Statute of the Courts, as are a few non-members like Switzerland and the tiny Liechtenstein. The authority of the Court covers any international issue submitted to it either by the voluntary act of some particular state or by the

United Nations itself. It has no power to impose or enforce its decisions but some thirty-six states, including Britain, have now agreed to recognise as compulsory the jurisdiction of the Court in all legal disputes concerning the interpretation of a treaty or any debatable question of international law. The Court has fifteen judges of high judicial and legal qualifications who are elected by the General Assembly and the Security Council and who serve for nine-year periods. The Headquarters of the Court is in the Peace Palace at The Hague in the Netherlands.

The loneliest job

The Secretariat, which works in New York or Geneva or in the regional and field locations of the United Nations, is the working staff of the organisation and now forms an international civil service of some seven to eight thousand persons, reflecting in various proportions, almost all the nationalities represented in the United Nations itself. The Head of the Secretariat is the Secretary-General who is appointed by the General Assembly on the recommendation of the Security Council and who, in turn, appoints the staff of the organisation under regulations laid down by the Assembly. Those who are appointed to the Secretariat do not surrender their nationality but they are pledged not to receive instructions from any outside authority in the work of the organisation. They are international civil servants answerable only to the United Nations. The main officials under the Secretary-General are now the eight Assistant Secretaries-General; the eleven Under-Secretaries and the Executive Secretaries of such agencies as the Children's Fund (UNICEF) and of the Regional Economic Commissions in Africa, Asia and elsewhere, and the Director of the European office in Geneva. To date, there have been three Secretaries-General of the organisation; the first Trygve Lie, a Norwegian; the second a Swede, Dag Hammarskjold who died while still in office as the result of an airplane disaster in Africa, and the present occupant of the post, U Thant, a Burmese, who is now in his second term of office. The Secretary-General, holds 'the loneliest and most responsible job in the world'.

From League to United Nations
We suggested earlier that though the United Nations was
built on broadly the same pattern as the League of Nations, it
would be a mistake to regard the new organisation as simply
a continuance of the old. Even in the constitutions of the two
bodies—the Covenant of the League and the Charter of the
United Nations—there are differences which are not just
verbal. Lessons had been learnt both from the collapse of the
League and from the dire events that followed. Beyond this,
there have been differences in the emphasis placed by the two
organisations on this or that aspect of their work, as we shall
see when we consider the tremendous range of the economic
and social activity to which the United Nations is now committed. Above all, there is the marked contrast in membership
between the two bodies which has made the United Nations a
very different organisation in character and outlook from
the old League.

At the outset, it is true, the membership of the United
Nations had broadly the same kind of geographical spread as
the old League of Nations. Thirty-six of the fifty-one founding
states came from Europe and the Americas and only thirteen
came from Africa, the Middle East and Asia. But within
fifteen years the pattern of membership in the United Nations
had been transformed by the entry, first of the former enemy
and neutral states of the Second World War, and then of the
whole troop of countries which have become independent
between 1955 and today. Now there are more than forty
states in the United Nations from Africa alone. Of the total
membership of one hundred and twenty-six states, some sixty
states, virtually half, come, in fact, from the two continents
of Africa and Asia. The United Nations is still not a universal
body in the complete sense, and will not become so until at
least the People's Republic of China with its seven hundred
million people, finds its place within the organisation. But
there is no question that its membership is much more
comprehensive and diverse than the membership of the
former League. This diversity will further increase as an
anticipated twenty or more eligible territories enter the
organisation in the next decade.

Changing patterns

So much then for the structure and composition of the United Nations, its similarities to and differences from the old League, and the general aims for which it was established. These aims were twofold; in the broadest terms they were, on the one hand, the prevention of war and the settlement of disputes that lead to war, and on the other the development of the kind of world, in economic and social terms, in which wars and conflicts are less likely to occur. The two aims, as we have already emphasised, cannot be sharply separated; they are part of the one purpose of creating a peaceful and prosperous human society. But it is convenient to separate them in this analysis of the achievements of the United Nations in the quarter of a century that has elapsed since 1945.

Preventing war

To-date, the third world war—the war, that is to say, between two or more of the world's super-powers—has not occurred. It would have destroyed the United Nations if it had occurred, and is likely to do so, if it occurs in future. The United Nations has made some contribution to the avoidance of war between the great powers but it has not been the decisive influence. The decisive factor has been a sharply realistic sense of the certain consequences of a great-power war fought, as is at least a possibility, with thermo-nuclear weapons; the recognition, that is to say, by the great powers that any open military conflict between them could engulf and virtually destroy the world. But if there has been no war of world-wide dimensions in the last twenty-five years there have been, as we saw in Chapter One, plenty of lesser wars, not insignificant for those involved in them and all the time, carrying within them the possibility of wider conflicts. Repeatedly over the years, the United Nations has intervened in wars of this magnitude to bring hostilities to an end and to encourage the combatants to resolve their differences by peaceful means. We shall see what has been achieved by this kind of intervention as we look at the situations in the Middle East, in the Congo, in Cyprus and elsewhere where the United Nations has stepped in.

The Korean war

In view of all the difficulties, it is surprising that so much has been achieved by the United Nations in this field. The first test came in June, 1950 when North Korean armies moved across the 38th Parallel to attack South Korea and penetrated deeply into South Korean territory. The 38th Parallel had been established after the defeat of the Japanese in the Second World War, with the implied agreement of the United States and the Soviet Union, as the temporary frontier between North and South Korea, pending the re-unification of the whole of Korea, a reunification which, in fact, still awaits realisation twenty-five years later. As the North Korean armies plunged deep into Korea, the Security Council in New York declared this a breach of the peace, called for an end to hostilities and began the organisation of the collective force, under the formal authority of the United Nations, which fought for virtually three years to drive the North Koreans out of South Korea and to establish in July, 1953 an Armistice agreement and an uneasy peace between the two sides which continues to this day. In name this was a United Nations action to repel and defeat aggression and some twenty states sent combatant units to fight in Korea. But the great bulk of the troops fighting under the United Nations flag were American and the strategic direction of the war was in the hands of American commanders in the field and American planners in the United States. In no sense, then, can this be called a typical intervention by the United Nations.

The Middle East

The second grave threat to the peace involving the United Nations, occurred in July, 1956 when Egypt nationalised the Suez Canal Company—hitherto under the control of the British and French governments—and took the management of the Canal which runs through Egyptian territory, into its own hands. Attempts to reach a peaceful solution of the crisis satisfactory to Britain and France having failed, these two countries together with Israel, invaded Egypt 'in defence of vital national interests' and later began air attacks against

Egyptian military targets. Replying to these attacks, the Egyptians sank ships in the Canal, closing this major international waterway for the first time in its history.

Divisions among the great powers prevented the Security Council taking direct action to restore peace but the General Assembly set itself to stop the fighting and secure the withdrawal of the invading armies from Egypt. It also began to create an international force under United Nations command to secure and supervise the cease-fire demanded in its resolutions and, faced with these decisions and actions and by a rising tide of hostile world opinion, Britain, France and Israel accepted the cease-fire demand of the United Nations and withdrew their forces from Egyptian soil. The United Nations Emergency Force which was later sent to Palestine was composed at the outset of some six thousand men, drawn from ten countries, including Brazil, Canada, India and Norway, and commanded by a Canadian, General Burns. Established in 'the Gaza strip' in Palestine and along the international frontier between Egypt and Israel, this small body of men kept the peace in this area for nearly eleven years without firing a single shot. The force was disbanded in June, 1967 on the eve of the six-day war between Israel and the Arab States, since it no longer seemed possible for it to stay on Egyptian territory once that country had insisted on its withdrawal. So ended, perhaps the most successful experiment of the United Nations up to this time in the use of an international 'police' force to keep the peace in a troubled land.

Anarchy in the Congo
Two other major experiments in international peacekeeping by the United Nations remain to be mentioned. The first of these tells a less encouraging story because the United Nations, intervening to try and establish peace and order in a country that was falling into anarchy, became unwillingly involved in military hostilities. One week after the Congo, a former Belgian-ruled territory in Central Africa, had become independent in June 1960, a mutiny occurred in the country's national army and grave acts of violence were committed

Officers of the U.N. Military Force in the Congo

against remaining Belgian officers and civilians. There was a mass flight of Belgian administrators from the Congo and a breakdown of essential services in many areas. Uninvited by the Congolese Government, Belgian troops were flown in from Europe to protect the lives and property of Belgian citizens and in the general chaos Moise Tshombe, head of government in the major province of Katanga, took the opportunity to declare the independence of his region. Within a week, the central Government had asked the United Nations to send military forces to protect the national territory of the Congo against external 'aggression'—the re-occupation by the Belgians—and to remove a threat to international peace. Within two days of a decision by the Security Council to call for the withdrawal of Belgian forces and to provide the Congolese government with the military and technical United Nations aid it needed to re-establish order within the country, the first United Nations contingent made up of troops from a wide variety of nations, landed in Leopoldville as the nucleus of a force eventually to number 20,000 men. The photo above shows U.N. officers from Nigeria, Denmark, Canada and Argentina.

A United Nations peace force

So far the declared aims of the United Nations in the Congo had been achieved without resort to fighting. Katanga had been entered by the United Nations forces but the threat of the province to separate itself from the rest of the Congo remained. The United Nations made clear that it was not its business to intervene in a country's internal conflicts but its forces did engage in the rounding-up of Tshombe's mercenaries in Katanga and it was in the course of these operations in September, 1961 that the United Nations troops were attacked by Katanganese *gendarmerie*. Three weeks elapsed before the fighting stopped and a cease-fire was secured. Meanwhile Dag Hammarskjold, the Secretary-General of the United Nations, intervening personally to try and stop the fighting, had been killed in the service of peace when the aeroplane in which he was flying to Ndola, crashed. Later, violence broke out again; United Nations personnel were attacked, abducted and killed. More than a year was to pass before peace was established in Katanga with the declared readiness of President Tshombe to end Katanganese secession and to cooperate with the United Nations in carrying out a Plan of National Reconciliation.

This was the most controversial, and in all senses the most costly, of the interventions the United Nations has undertaken for the sake of peace. Doubtless, errors were made in a unique and complicated operation but it is not difficult to imagine how grave would have been the danger to world peace in the summer of 1960, if there had been no United Nations to step into the Congo situation and the way had been left open for the rival interventions of the great powers. In any case, throughout the political crises and the military actions the United Nations, through its civilian operations, was reorganising the public services, restoring the shattered economy and through its famine relief activities in the Kasai province, saving the lives of a quarter of a million Congolese.

The Cyprus question

Our last example of this role of the United Nations takes us to the Eastern Mediterranean, to Cyprus. The problem of Cyprus, and of peace in Cyprus, is centred in the fact that four-fifths of its people are of Greek origin and Orthodox Christians by religion, while the remaining fifth are of Turkish origin and of the Moslem faith. From the nineteen thirties onwards, the rivalries of these two unequal national groups, intensified by Greek Cypriot agitation for union with Greece, faced the British administrators with mounting unrest, frequent violence and on occasions, open war. From 1954 onwards, the Cyprus question was constantly before the United Nations on the initiative of Greece or Turkey or of Great Britain herself. Eventually in 1959, Cyprus became by agreement of Britain, Greece and Turkey, an independent republic to be governed jointly by Greek and Turkish Cypriots, and eighteen months later became a member of the United Nations, but neither event brought peace to the island or a final solution of its problems.

From 1961 onwards, one political crisis followed another; the cooperation of the two peoples in the government became increasingly unworkable and a Greek campaign to settle the problem by force which led to the seizure of Turkish hostages and the murder of Turks in their homes, led to the stationing of a joint British, Greek and Turkish force along the so-called 'green lines' dividing the two communities. In March 1964, these troops were replaced by a U.N. Force made up of some 6,500 troops from Canada, Britain, Ireland, Finland, Sweden, Denmark and Austria. Supporting the troops were 175 civilian police, coming from broadly the same countries.

This force has now been in Cyprus for six years or more—though on a very uncertain basis latterly because of shortage of funds to meet its costs—and is still there today. The number of troops fell to little more than 3,000 in 1968, though the number of civilian police remained the same. Like all United Nations forces its primary task is to keep the peace and to use force, as far as possible, only in self-defence. It has suffered a few casualties in its own ranks but, for the most part, has been a model illustration of what international peace-keeping or international police work, under the United Nations can achieve. It can be given credit for the fact that, considering the explosive situation that has existed in Cyprus, the level of violence there has, on the whole, been kept remarkably low. There is still no final solution in sight in Cyprus but that is not the fault of the United Nations troops who are there not to settle the Cyprus problem but to maintain peace and order and to provide the conditions in which a political settlement may eventually be reached.

Unarmed observers

This is the story, then, of the United Nations acting as a kind of international fire-brigade; the story of the steps taken by the United Nations, either to stop wars or prevent small wars becoming bigger wars, or to create some semblance of order where orderly government has broken down. But the peace-keeping functions, as they are called, of the United Nations are not limited to the sending of international armed forces into troubled areas. It may not be practicable or even necessary for the United Nations to organise an international armed force of this character, and even if it is practicable, the financial means or the political will may not be there to enable it to do so. Apart from this, the United Nations has other steps it can take to reduce the tension in a given crisis, to prevent disputes leading to open conflict, and limited wars growing into larger wars. It can send unarmed observers into conflict situations to gather information on which further action by the United Nations can be based or to supervise a cease-fire, once an agreement to stop fighting has been made. By using its resources for mediation or by exerting political and moral pressure through the Security Council and the Assembly, it can secure a cease-fire without involving itself directly in the situation through the despatch of an international force. Especially when the great powers themselves are involved in some major crisis, it can provide the means whereby the risks of a direct confrontation between them can be reduced and a way out of the crisis found without humiliation for either side.

Though it was not, in the main, action by the United Nations which resolved the grave crisis over the stationing of Russian missiles in Cuba in 1963, the United Nations played an important part in reducing tension and lessening the imminent risks of world war.

No mean achievement

Taking all in all, this is no mean record of achievement for the United Nations in the peace-keeping field. To have lessened the risk of world war in one major crisis between the great powers, would be ample justification for having a United Nations and for its continuing existence in a world threatened always by the immeasurable disaster of global nuclear war. But as the evidence shows, the direct intervention of the United Nations in what we choose to call lesser conflicts, has saved many millions of people the world over from the scourge of war and confirmed its role as the only international guardian of the peace. The United Nations has been less successful, it must be said, in following up its intervention to stop fighting, with effective measures to secure a peaceful settlement of the dispute itself, even when only smaller countries are involved. But though this is a vital part of the United Nations' responsibility, success in which may be critical for the future of the United Nations itself, it is a much more difficult task to perform. The United Nations can in the last resort compel at least smaller states to stop fighting. It cannot so easily—if at all—compel disputants to make peace. And only too frequently its failure to do this is not so much a failure of the organisation itself, but a reflection of the unwillingness, or the inability, of the great powers to agree that a peaceful settlement of the dispute is desirable and to pool their influence to achieve it.

TOPICS FOR DISCUSSION

- The United Nations has only partially achieved its purpose of 'saving succeeding generations from the scourge of war'. What are the obstacles it has had to face in carrying out this task?

- What sort of steps could be taken to strengthen the United Nations so that it becomes, if not a world government, at least a body with more authority to prevent fighting and to ensure that disputes are settled peacefully?

9

The thousand common ventures

From the beginning, as we have seen, the United Nations undertook not only to stop war and aggression but to create progressively the kind of world in which war and aggression became less likely and in which the word peace would begin to have some positive meaning. We have noted that one of the major organs of the United Nations, the Economic and Social Council, was set up to fulfil this purpose and in our consideration of the crisis of world poverty, we acknowledged the contribution made to the narrowing of the gap between the rich and the poor nations by the United Nations Conferences on Trade and Development. In this chapter we take a broader look at these social and humanitarian activities of the United Nations, this varied effort to build up the common life of the world.

Even though the founders of the United Nations saw from the outset the close relation between peace and social justice and built this principle into the structure and programmes of the organisation, they could scarcely have dreamed how much of the time and energy of their United Nations would be devoted over the years to its economic and social objectives. This work for international social welfare rarely gains the newspaper headlines, but it absorbs more than four-fifths of the personnel and resources of the United Nations system. It is not work that is to be seen as standing alone; it cannot be isolated from the political conditions in which it has to be carried out and the international tensions which only too often hinder its progress. But in a fundamental sense, it represents the most solid and hopeful form of peace-making. 'World order will come', said Adlai Stevenson in one of the last of his speeches as American delegate to the United Nations, 'not through the purity of the human heart nor the purge of the human soul but will be wrought from a thousand common ventures that are at once possible and imperative.'

A complex structure

The 'thousand common ventures' in the economic and social field involve, not only a small army of international civil servants but a wide range of agencies and organisations. Beyond or beneath the Economic and Social Council and the relevant committees of the General Assembly, are seven specialised commissions dealing with specific problems of world-wide importance such as population growth, the safeguarding of human rights, the enhancement of the status of women, and the control of the traffic in narcotic drugs. Beyond these 'functional' commissions are four regional economic commissions, based on Geneva, Bangkok, Santiago and Addis Ababa and set up to deal with the economic problems and needs of Europe, Asia and the Far East, Latin America and Africa. Beyond these still, are the fourteen so-called specialised agencies (including the International Atomic Energy Authority which is not strictly a specialised Agency) which are separate, self-governing organisations linked with the United Nations as the plan on page 110 indicates, and financed by it under special and individual arrangements. Some of these agencies existed even before the United Nations; one of them, the International Labour Organisation, was actually a part of the League of Nations system. Most of the others had their origins, as we noted in the previous chapter, in the inter-allied organisations set up in the later stage of the Second World War.

All this is machinery, the bare bones as it were, of the functional activity of the United Nations. To give reality to the needs which the machinery exists to serve, we have to identify ourselves in feeling and imagination with the child dying of starvation or under-nourishment in an Indian or Peruvian village, or of yaws in Indonesia or enduring preventable blindness in an African kraal. We have to translate the names and the functions of organisations into the thousand ventures—the multitude of practical, though often trivial-looking, tasks which bring world responsibility and the complexities of international action right down to the needy and suffering individual. We have to think of the medical expert testing the mosquito tents set up in the malaria-infested areas of Africa and Asia; of the worker building the dam for the irrigation project in the Mekong Valley of South-East Asia; of the white-coated food technician in an institute in Guatemala trying to improve the nutritional quality of the tortilla cakes, made from cornflour, which are the staple diet of the villagers of Central America. We have to think of the internationally-financed doctor working to free Africans from the threat of leprosy, or of the child-care worker looking after children amidst the desolation of the war in Vietnam. We have to think of the boys in the remote village of Afghanistan who would have no education at all without international assistance, or of the villagers laying a vital water pipeline under an internationally-sponsored project in an African community.

The major scourges
This is United Nations social and economic betterment in action. To describe it, even in outline, in all its aspects would be beyond the scope and purpose of our study. But if we assume that (together with war) hunger, disease and illiteracy are the major scourges of mankind, we can gain some idea of the significance of the contribution which the world organisation is making in the field of social welfare, if we look at the actions taken by the United Nations to deal with these three enemies and to help supply the basic human needs of food, health and education.

The basic fact of the world food situation is that over-all food production is not keeping pace with the growth of population; always there are more mouths to feed and less food to put in them. The third World Survey, issued in 1963 by the Food and Agriculture Organisation, estimated that while the quantity and quality of average world diets had improved a little since 1945, ten to fifteen per cent of the world's people (about 400 million persons) were undernourished and even hungry and up to one-half of them (about 1·5 thousand million people) were suffering from malnutrition.

Since 1963, though there has been a small but steady increase in world agricultural output, world population has increased by more than sixty-one million people each year, so

that production per head of population has hardly changed
(see the map below.) United Nations experts in population
problems have calculated, as we noted in Chapter Three,
that the population of the world which was only 1·5 thousand
million in 1900, will approach 7,000 million—more than
twice its present figure—by the year 2000. The World Survey
went on to estimate that food production would have to be
trebled if all the peoples alive in the year 2000 were to be
adequately fed. (Production did, in fact, rise by three per cent
in 1967, after two years of bad harvests.) The sale abroad of
American, Canadian and Australian wheat surpluses eased
or postponed the crisis for a time in some of the needier
countries but these are now virtually exhausted and cannot be
expected to recur. 'The world's foodbins', Lord Boyd-Orr,
the first Director-General of the Food and Agriculture
Organisation has said in a graphic phrase 'are empty'.

Some hopeful factors
Refilling the bins and above all keeping them full, is an
immense task and there is no certainty that it can be achieved

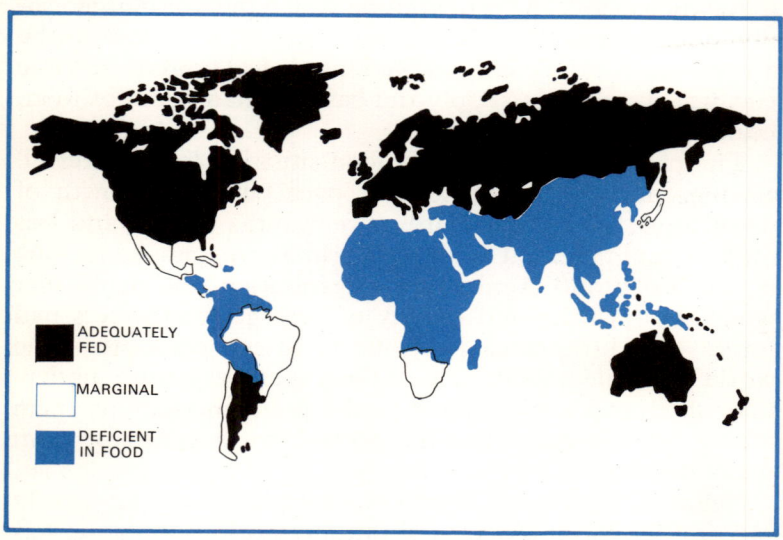

The geography of hunger—1968

in time, or sufficiently to arrest the threatened crisis. But there is some comfort to be had from the fact that as the problem grows, so do the means of resolving it. Technology is providing the tools to solve the problem if men can be given the skills to use them. Science is constantly developing new species of plants and of livestock which give larger yields; new machinery and more modern methods of farming enable more food to be produced with less human effort; new techniques, even in fishing, increase the productivity of the fishing-grounds which, in this case, is growing faster than world population, and enable the fish to be got more rapidly to the consumer. For years famine has been a commonplace on the Indian sub-continent but recently farmers have started using larger quantities of improved cereal varieties and fertiliser to produce harvests in 1967 and 1968 that broke all records. Brian Silcock writing on 'The overflowing rice bowl' in India and Pakistan, described the new-found varieties of rice and wheat—'tailor-made for the tropics' as 'the spearhead of this new agricultural revolution'. Bred with painstaking care from existing varieties, collected from all over the world, these new varieties are enabling farmers to double and treble the amount of grain they can harvest from a single piece of land. The Indian sub-continent, it was suggested, might even become within a few years, a net exporter of grain. All this is encouraging, though the speed at which it can take full effect must not be exaggerated. The Food and Agriculture Organisation's Annual Report for 1968, warned against over-optimism:

> It would be a mistake to jump to the conclusion that the world food problem has been solved either temporarily or permanently. Realising the new potential will not be easy. . . .

Beyond this, more is being learnt through scientific experimentation about nutritional requirements for health and survival. Dietary standards throughout the world are being steadily improved and approaches are being made to the preparation of manufactured proteins, fats and carbohydrates which could supplement and, in time, even become competitive with natural food. 'If food shortage' said Dr Magnus Pyke, a research chemist, 'rather than a shortage of copper, paper or space, does become the limiting factor in the human race, food can undoubtedly be synthesised in chemical factories at a price.'

The Food and Agriculture Organisation
The problem, therefore, is not what to do to avert a world food crisis but to ensure that it is done. Internationally the main instrument of action is the Food and Agriculture Organisation—a specialised agency of the United Nations located in Rome, which has a staff of some 2,700 people (five thousand if field officers and experts are included) and had in 1968, a usable income from all sources to cover both its regular and field activities, of about thirty-three million pounds a year. The Food and Agriculture Organisation (F.A.O.) was established in 1945 as the outcome of a world food conference held at Hot Springs in the United States. Beginning with the modest roles of consultation and information, it soon launched itself into the campaign against world hunger, utilising a major share of United Nations funds available for technical assistance to developing countries. It was providing by 1965, some 1,300 technical experts of all nationalities working in ninety countries. Their responsibility was not to do the necessary tasks themselves but to advise, guide and train citizens of the country to do them. Under these programmes, experts from F.A.O. trained, for example, Ceylonese fishermen in mechanised fishing, helped the Egyptians to double their production of rice, aided the improvement of the Mexican poultry industry and the setting up of new paper industries in Asia and Latin America, trained nutrition workers in the West Indies and planted fruit trees in Indonesia. Once the United Nations had established its Special Fund for the financing of major development projects, F.A.O. became the executive agency for a wide variety of projects sponsored by the Fund—keeping, for example, sea-water out of a 60,000 square kilometer sweet-water lagoon in Brazil and Uruquay and planning a watershed scheme in Venezuela to irrigate 1·5 million hectares of arid soil.

The F.A.O.'s programme has been given greater force in recent years with the establishment in 1963 of the World Food

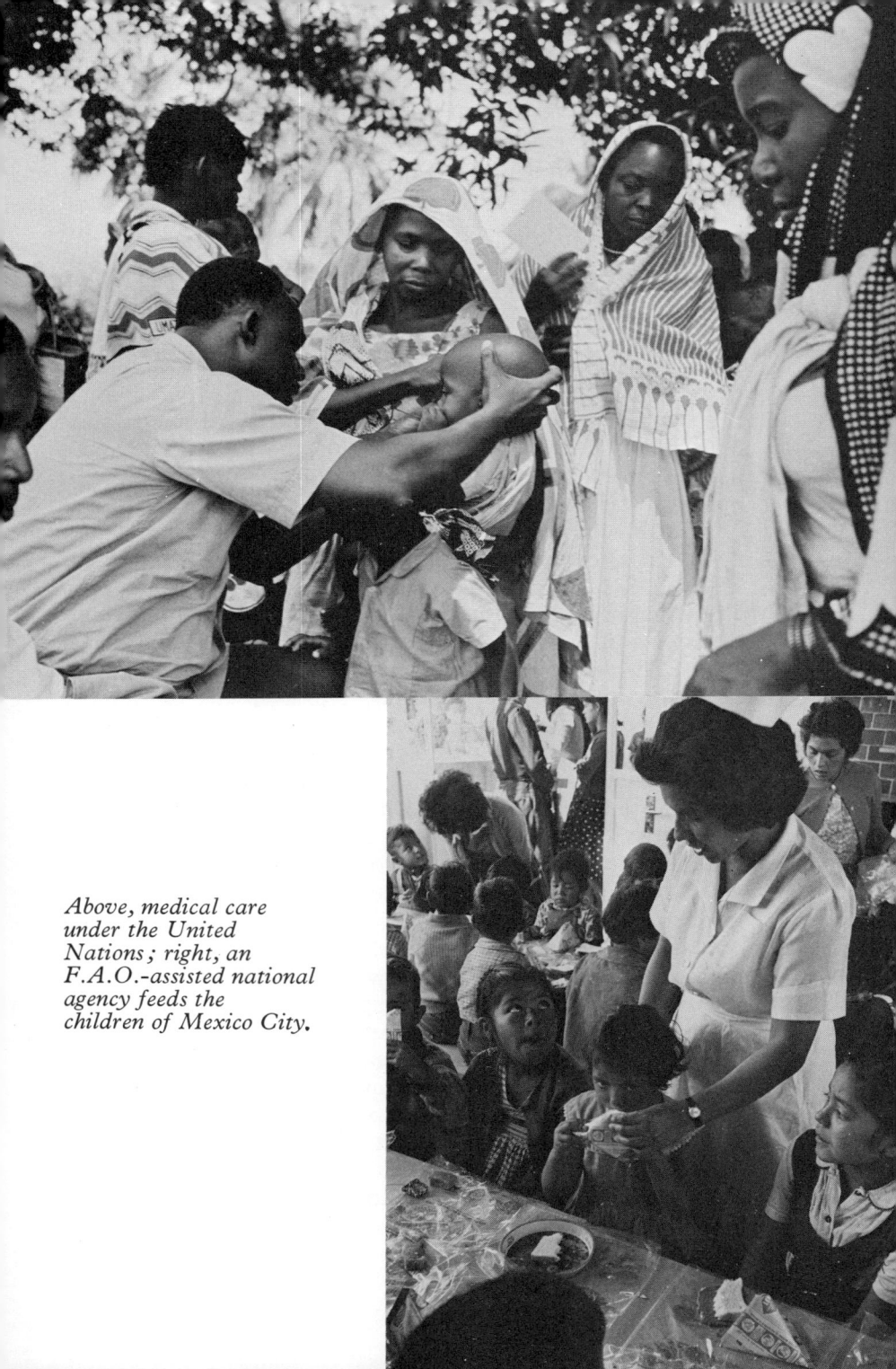

Above, medical care under the United Nations; right, an F.A.O.-assisted national agency feeds the children of Mexico City.

Programme, and of a Cooperative Programme with the World Bank in 1964. The World Food Programme, which F.A.O. administers jointly with the United Nations, uses food supplies pledged by member governments not only for disaster relief but also as a sort of finance for development programmes. For example, food is used to pay workers digging irrigation channels to create new farmlands or to plant trees on hillsides to check erosion. By the end of 1967 the World Food Programme had agreed to back 264 development projects in 64 countries at an overall cost of one hundred and two million pounds. Through the Cooperative Programme with the World Bank, F.A.O. helps the Bank to increase investment in agriculture by bringing suitable investment opportunities to the Bank's notice. Largely as a consequence of this cooperation the Bank invested a record total of eighty million pounds in agricultural development in 1967 alone.

The menace of disease
If, after war, hunger can be reckoned man's chief social enemy, disease runs a close second. Hunger and disease, indeed, run in double harness. Millions succumb more readily to disease because of undernourishment and malnutrition. Disease, in turn, threatens not only the individual but the whole economic life of a people, making it harder for them to develop their resources and help themselves to greater prosperity. A world food programme is essential to world health but food alone cannot conquer or eradicate disease; the direct, as well as the indirect attack on disease has to be made.

In the advanced countries, this direct attack already has considerable achievements to its credit. Life for early man was not only brutish but short; he was fortunate if he lived for thirty years. Today average life-expectancy in some parts of the Western world has reached seventy-five years—five years beyond the scriptural three score years and ten—for women and seventy years for men. For centuries, plague was a recurring feature in Western Europe. Between a third and a half of the people of England were victims of the Black Death of the fourteenth century. 50,000 people died of plague in Marseilles in 1770. As late as the nineteenth century, Europe suffered not only from plague but from cholera, leprosy, malaria, typhus and even yellow fever. In the advanced countries the development of public health services brought these diseases under control long before modern drugs were discovered. In the poor world the story is different. There the fight has begun in earnest but it still has to be won. One example, using the life expectancy measurement again, will suffice. In the period 1960–61, life expectancy at birth for males in Gabon (West Africa) was as low as twenty-five years.

It has long been recognised that disease knows no frontiers and international cooperation in promoting health and preventing disease began more than a century ago. The first International Sanitary Conference met in Paris in 1851. A regional health organisation known as the Pan-American Sanitary Bureau was set up in Washington in 1902, and five years later an international office of Public Health was established in Paris to keep records of diseases requiring quarantine and to recommend to governments measures for prevention and cure.

The World Health Organisation

As in other fields of human welfare, a major break-through in international cooperation in matters of health and disease came with the setting-up of the United Nations and the creation in 1948 of the World Health Organisation. Twenty-six originating member-nations gave the W.H.O. the ambitious objective of 'the attainment by all peoples of the highest level of health'—health being defined in the constitution of W.H.O. as 'a state of complete physical, mental and social well-being and not merely the absence of disease and infirmity.' Today, with headquarters in Geneva, it has 127 Member-States and four Associate Members and a team of 4,400 public servants, doctors, nurses and technicians drawn from ninety-two different nationalities, who carry out the programmes of the organisation, not only at headquarters but in 140 countries and territories throughout the world. Apart from its regular workers, it has some 2,500 scientists, health administrators and educationalists who can be called on by the Director-General to give expert advice on matters within their special fields. The task of providing direct assistance to national health administrations is decentralised through six regional offices situated in Brazzaville, for Africa; in Washington, for the Americas; in New Delhi, for south-east Asia; in Alexandria, for the Eastern Mediterranean; in Manila, for the Western Pacific and in Copenhagen for Europe. For all its operations, the W.H.O. has available an annual sum of roughly £32 million, but this includes the budgets of several subsidiary or related bodies such as the Pan-American Health Organisation.

The World Health Organisation has some twenty major functions, ranging from the formulation of international health conventions and regulations to the organisation of measures to promote mental health. A summary of its activities in a few selected fields, will show the scope and variety of its operations. Malaria is the most expensive and extensive world disease today; it still causes more deaths than any other disease as well as vast suffering and economic loss. Four hundred million people are still exposed to the disease but since 1955, when the W.H.O. set itself to abolish malaria nearly a thousand million people have been freed from its attack and the eradication programme still goes effectively forward in eighty-five countries. Eighty per cent of the people living in originally malarious areas are now protected.

Despite 150 years of vaccination there were 122,098 cases of smallpox in 1967 and nearly ten thousand deaths. The disease remains endemic in most of Africa south of the Sahara and in south-east Asia, where seventy per cent of the world's cases recur. Under an intensified and world-wide campaign to conquer smallpox begun in 1967, over 200 million vaccinations were given in the first year. Though polluted water supplies cause dysentry, typhoid, cholera and other diseases, ten per cent of the people in the developing areas still lack safe water in adequate supply. The world over, more than 200 million people lack good drinking water and to help reduce this number, the W.H.O. is assisting a number of countries in the improvement of water supply and waste disposal systems, as well as training sanitary engineers, chemists and bacteriologists. To combat tuberculosis, the organisation has extended

Above, a reading lesson in Nepal; below, combating malaria—
a United Nations aerial assault on the mosquito in the Congo

the mass immunisation campaign, started by Scandinavian Red Cross Societies after the Second World War, under which 200 million people in 61 countries have now been treated.

An expert W.H.O. Committee on addiction or dependence-producing drugs, is cooperating with the United Nations Commission on Narcotic Drugs and the International Narcotics Control Board to prevent the misuse of drugs through their diversion from legal to illegal channels of distribution and to ensure that narcotics control in one country, is not stultified by a lack of control in another. By 1965, the consumption of narcotic drugs had been reduced to half its previous extent but the flow of illicit traffic—mainly in opium, morphine, heroin and cannabis—is increasing again, and constant international vigilance is required to keep it under control. Prompted by the tragedy of the thalidomide babies, the W.H.O. has organised a system for monitoring the hundreds of new drugs which come on the market each year.

Saving the children

Children are specially vulnerable to disease and there is growing cooperation between the W.H.O. and the United Nations Children's Fund (UNICEF) in helping the thousand million growing children in the world to become happy and healthy citizens. Thirty thousand children die every day of preventable diseases; every year more than sixteen million babies die before they are one; intestinal infections—malaria, yaws, trachoma, leprosy and rickets—take a heavy toll of children though not all of these are killing diseases. In some developing countries, three-quarters of the children have tuberculosis before they are fourteen.

The Children's Fund in conjunction with the W.H.O. provides drugs, insecticides, antibiotics and vaccines, together with equipment and vehicles for mass campaigns to control these and other diseases. It helps countries to set up child welfare clinics and provides essential supplies for health, nutrition, education and vocational training. It gives emergency help including medical supplies and blankets, to the child victims of floods, earthquakes, drought and other natural disasters. Its aid to child nutrition programmes in twenty countries (which contribute an equivalent amount of aid themselves) was alone valued at £1·5 million in 1969–70. The work of UNICEF is not financed on the regular budget of the United Nations, but by voluntary gifts from governments, non-official organisations and individuals. Nowhere is the value of the welfare service of the United Nations more fully vindicated than in these labours for the citizen of tomorrow.

The war on ignorance

H. G. Wells once described human history as 'a race between education and catastrophe.' In the age of nuclear weapons, when man through scientific research and educational knowledge has gained the power to destroy his own civilisation, the remark takes on an unconscious irony. But the truth of the statement stands; whatever the dangers of the misuse of knowledge, there can be no continuing and generalised progress without it. Education, defined as the pursuit of knowledge and the ability to assimilate and use it, remains, to quote a phrase once used by the Director-General of UNESCO, 'a universal priority.'

Education is now accepted, therefore, as not only a fundamental human right but as a vital factor in economic and social development. Pope Paul VI in his historic Encyclical Letter of March, 1967 on the *Development of Peoples (Progressio Populorum)* which appealed for a crusade to free the world from social injustice, described 'the hunger for education—the lack of education—as no less debasing than the hunger for food.' An illiterate person, said the Encyclical, 'is a person with an undernourished mind.' Responding to this appeal, the Director-General of UNESCO, in the same comment quoted above, said that once it is realised that the only development worth the name 'is that of man through man and for man, it becomes clear that education, science and culture are the foundation and the culmination, the driving-force and the justifying end of development in its essence. It has been said that development is a state of mind; we might go further and say that development is the human mind on the march in history.'

The challenge of illiteracy
Education is much more than the ability to read and write
but these are the basic and essential skills of the educational
process. Illiteracy—the inability to use these skills—is a
major world problem. Almost half the world's children do not
go to school and more than 800 million people over fifteen
years of age (34% of the world's adult population) cannot
write or read. If the calculation is made on the basis of the
functionally illiterate—that is those unable to read or write
well enough to take an active part in a literate community, the
figure is thought to be nearer 65%. In some of the countries of
Asia, Africa and Latin America, illiteracy is as high as 75–90%
of the people and every year as the uneducated grow up, a
further twenty million people are added to the mass of
illiterates. The Universal Declaration of Human Rights which
in Article 26 recognises the right to education, can in fact be
read by only two people out of five the world over.

The international spear-head in the war on illiteracy is the
United Nations Educational, Scientific and Cultural Organisation (popularly known as UNESCO) which came to birth in
1946, to encourage educational, scientific and cultural
progress and to foster world-wide cooperation in all these
fields. On the principle enshrined in its constitution, that
'since wars begin in the minds of men, it is in the minds of men
that the defences of peace must be constructed', UNESCO
has undertaken a wide range of projects all designed to encourage international intellectual cooperation, to promote
mutual understanding between the peoples and a better
knowledge of their different cultures. In the educational field,
it gives advice and expert assistance in teacher-training, school-
building and the preparation of curricula and text books; it is
the world's clearing-house for information and documentation
in all aspects of education. In the field of science, UNESCO
helps its Member-States to improve the teaching of basic
science at all levels from the primary school to the university.

UNESCO's projects based on the international cooperation
of scientists have included a research expedition to the Indian
Ocean, in which more than twenty nations shared, and the
launching in 1965, of the International Hydrological Decade

in which scientists from 103 countries are now researching into the problems of water resources so as to bring back to life the parched and treeless territories, in what are known as the world's arid zones. In the field of the social sciences, UNESCO is delving into the social implications of rapid, technical change and into the problems of race and racial tension. Its work for a developed appreciation of different cultures, ranges from the support of an International Theatre Institute to the spectacular rescue operation to save the ancient monuments of Nubia from the rising waters of the Nile. In the field of communication, UNESCO organises schools for the training of journalists, promotes the cultural exchange of people and information, and encourages the contribution of the 'Mass Media' of newspapers, wireless and television, to international cooperation and understanding.

Prisoners of darkness

'At a time when science is opening a gateway to the stars it is unthinkable', said the executive head of UNESCO, 'that two-fifths of mankind should be prisoners of ancestral darkness.' UNESCO's plan for the liberation of the prisoners has the two-fold aim of providing more schools and of ending illiteracy. In Middle or 'Black' Africa, where about 80% of the people are illiterate and only two in a thousand children can hope to go to college or university (to take one example only, Zambia at independence had only 900 Africans with a completed secondary education) UNESCO is helping in the operation of twenty teacher-training colleges at the secondary level—one only of more than a hundred education development projects in thirty-two African countries. In Asia, nineteen countries are cooperating in an educational programme which is trying to ensure that by 1980, there will be enough schools and teachers to enable all 200 million of their primary school children to be educated.

UNESCO's campaign against illiteracy which was begun in 1963 with a world-wide objective, was focused experimentally on seven countries where literacy campaigns have been started as an integral part of the social development of the area. By the end of 1968, UNESCO had sent advisory missions on functional literacy projects to over forty other countries. And since experience shows that the newly-literate adult forgets what he has learnt within a month, unless he has the means to continue reading and to sustain his interest in the knowledge he is gaining, the campaign not only teaches him to read and write but provides him with the reading material which his new-found literacy demands. Even so, there is little change yet to be seen in the size and significance of the problem. In 1950, there were 700 million illiterates out of a total of 1,579 million adults; by 1970 there could be 810 million. If UNESCO is not to be fighting a battle it must lose, greater resources still need to be put into its literacy campaign.

We have taken these efforts of the United Nations and its allied agencies to combat hunger, disease and illiteracy, as samples only of the work that is being done through international organisations to provide the conditions of economic and social progress for all the peoples. But any complete record of the work of the United Nations, and its related agencies for social betterment, would need to note much more even than this. It would acknowledge what the International Atomic Energy Authority is doing to encourage the peaceful uses of atomic energy and, to take one surprising example, to apply nuclear techniques to the control of the Mediterranean fruit fly which causes immense losses by attacking citrus fruit, such as oranges, as well as peaches. It would mention the work of the International Labour Office and the International Civil Aviation Authority. It would recognise the unspectacular but vital work which the Universal Postal Union is doing, to enable virtually all countries to operate as a single postal territory, and to receive and send 3,000 million pieces of mail each year. It would recognise the work of the World Meteorological Organisation in developing weather-forecasting services through international cooperation and a rapid interchange of weather information.

All this and much more constitutes the welfare service of the United Nations—the activity that is designed to give a worthier life to the world's people. Two points about this functional work of the United Nations remain to be stressed. The first is the central importance of economic and industrial development in the countries concerned to the fulfilment of the programmes and purposes of the international welfare agencies of which we have been speaking. The under-nourished millions, the peoples suffering the ravages of disease, the peoples condemned, to recall M. Matheu's striking phrase, 'to ancestral darkness' live for the most part, as we have already noted, in the under-developed or developing areas of the world. They cannot make the best use of the efforts of international agencies to help them unless they can break out of the vicious circle of poverty and under-production and make their own economic way in the world.

One single purpose
The second point to be stressed, is the point made at the beginning of this chapter, which is that these economic and social programmes of the United Nations have to be seen as inseparably linked to the political purposes and the political fortunes of the United Nations. The truth is that in the longer run, the work of the United Nations—as of the League of Nations—will succeed or fail as a whole. However vital and worth-while the constructive peace-building work of the United Nations may be, it could not survive a continuing failure in the primary purpose of the organisation, the purpose of putting an end to war.

TOPICS FOR DISCUSSION

- Why is the social welfare of peoples so important a factor in creating a peaceful and orderly world?

- Are hunger, disease and ignorance rightly chosen as—after war—the major afflictions of mankind?

- To what extent are these welfare services of the United Nations mere palliatives, failing to touch problems which call for more radical solutions?

10

People and peace

No-one who has read so far will have failed to realise that, however vital it is to build an international society that has abandoned war as an instrument of national policy and found the peaceful way to settle its disputes and differences, the difficulties of doing this are formidable and the certainty of success by no means assured.

There are some who would say that the effort is bound to fail. There have been wars, it is said, since the dawn of history; there always will be wars since this is in the nature of things, and in the nature of the human person. The individual is naturally aggressive and must and will find outlets for his aggressive urges if not in open violence, at least in a militant self-assertiveness which only too often has scant regard for the rights and interests of others. Nations, the argument goes on, are only the individual writ large; they too must assert themselves to survive and seek by whatever means are available, to protect their rights and safeguard their interests against all comers. It is over-idealistic to assume, therefore— the argument runs—that this can be changed. The justification of war in these terms is perhaps unfashionable today, but it is not rare, and often unconsciously it colours much popular thinking on the problems of war and peace.

There are others who argue that war performs a function in society which society cannot do without and for which it would be difficult, if not impossible, to find satisfactory alternatives. There was published in the United States in 1967, a *Report from Iron Mountain* on the consequences of world peace, if ever attained, for the future stability of American society. The Report claimed to be a study prepared by a specialised group for a secret committee of the United States government, but the claim was disputed by most reviewers. The Report was generally assumed to be either the work of the book's Editor, Leonard Lewin, or of a so-called John Doe, from whom the Editor claimed to have received it.

The case for war

Whatever its origins, the Report set out with clarity and an impressive weight of evidence, the social justification for war in modern society. War, said the Report, is not simply an instrument of policy, used reluctantly by nations to defend their national or economic interests or their political values; war and the war system constitute the very basis on which all modern societies are built. War and preparation for war have provided both ancient and modern societies with a dependable system for maintaining and stabilising their economies. Though there has been much vague talk about converting an economy based substantially on the possibility of war and the production of arms, to an economy devoted wholly to 'peaceful' production, no convincing way of making the changeover, or of ensuring that the same results are achieved, has yet been worked out. Moreover, said the Report, the possibility of war is the mainstay of all stable government because it is this, in the last resort, which enables governments to maintain their authority over their people. Without some belief in the public mind that war or attack remains a possibility, governments might find it impossible to sustain their ruling power. Beyond this, the institutions and instruments of war, especially the armed forces of the state, serve to discourage popular revolt and to keep destructive and anti-social tendencies under control. It is war, moreover, the Report argued, that has helped to keep the balance between growing populations and the resources available to feed and sustain them. Finally, said the Report, it is war that, in the main, has provided the spur to scientific and technological progress.

The aggressive impulse

To take the argument about human nature first; it is not necessary to accept the theory of the inevitability of war to recognise that there are psychological factors in the problem of war and peace that have to be reckoned with by those who seek to build a warless world. No competent psychologist would deny that in the human make-up there are aggressive or assertive impulses that tend to find expression, sooner or later, in creative or destructive ways. These impulses sometimes lead to anti-social aggressiveness in the individual, but they can also be the source and inspiration of positive achievements in the field of discovery and invention, of scientific endeavour, of exploration and adventure. The task is not to seek to suppress them but to direct them to socially-useful ends and above all, since few can climb Everest or sail single-handed round the world, to bring to the day-to-day life of the individual something of the adventure, the danger and the sacrifice which war demands.

The argument of the *Report from Iron Mountain* calls for the same kind of response. It would be absurd to deny that war and the preparation for war, have stimulated economic and scientific progress and contributed to the social togetherness of modern societies and of the nation-state—however grim the other side of the balance-sheet of war may be in terms of material destruction and human suffering. To take one example alone: the First World War compelled Britain to undertake a massive industrial modernisation which might otherwise have been delayed for decades. Several of Britain's exporting industries owe their existence or their expansion to this war—for example chemicals, aero-engines, aircraft, motor vehicles, optical glass and photographic equipment. It is also true that not enough thought has been given to ways and means of achieving these same desirable social objectives without war, and in particular of transforming an economy geared to war to one geared to peace. But the answer is not to assume that war is eternally necessary for this purpose. It is to get on with the job of finding the substitute institutions as the *Report from Iron Mountain* calls them, and the substitute methods, which will ultimately displace the non-military functions and uses of war. This is an essential part of the constructive planning which true peace-making demands.

The threats to peace
We must then, if we are to survive in the age of thermo-nuclear armaments, reject the assumption that wars must always occur because the human animal is inherently aggressive or because modern societies like our own are incapable of preventing the dislocation or the anarchy that would ensue

if lasting peace 'broke out'. Nevertheless there are numerous problems and situations in the world today which, failing adequate steps to resolve or change them peacefully, make the recurrence of wars, whether minor or major, at least a proba- bility. We have considered them, in turn, in this book: the world poverty crisis, the clash of race and colour, the revival of militant nationalism in many places. All these threaten peace and order at the fundamental level and promise conflicts of growing intensity around the world. More immediately, only an uneasy truce prevents renewed fighting between Israel and its Arab neighbours in the Middle East, with little or no prospect of a settled peace. In Europe, an artificial frontier continues to divide the German people, and the beginning of the break-up of the Soviet overlordship in Eastern Europe creates new international dangers, even if it promises also the greater freedom which the peoples under communist rule desire and deserve. The increasing power of China casts, as we have said, a shadow over the whole future of world affairs. And finally, the United Nations has still to become the effective instrument of international security which might enable these problems to be settled by peaceful means.

Beneath all these particular problems and their possible solution, lies the deeper question as to how aggression, tyranny, and injustice are to be resisted and overcome without resort to war—without recourse to methods which, in this day and age, are singularly ill-fitted to produce justice and may even bring about the end of human history. The dilemma was well expressed by H. J. N. Horsburgh in a recent book on the teachings of M. K. Gandhi called *Non-Violence and Aggression.*

> Either we must renounce war and place ourselves at the mercy of those who care nothing for the values we cherish or we must prepare for a struggle that might destroy our civilisation and even annihilate our species. To acquiesce in the triumph of injustice seems intolerable: on the other hand the justice that can only be done by putting the heavens at serious risk, seems too rough to make much appeal to a responsible human being.

The answer still has to be found. The dilemma still has to be resolved, though perhaps in their faith in, and their demonstration of, the power of non-violence to overcome evil and achieve peaceful change, such men as Gandhi, Chief Luthuli, Martin Luther King and Albert Schweitzer have pointed the way.

No easy option

In these circumstances, only the wilfully blind or the incurably simple, could persuade themselves that peace is an easy option requiring only vague hopes and desultory action to bring it about. 'The war against war', said William James, 'is going to be no holiday excursion or camping party'. Learned men can argue and differ as to whether man in his basic nature is more peaceable than warlike or vice versa. What seems to be beyond argument is that war comes, if only by their inactions, a good deal more easily than peace, to men and nations. Peace-making is, in fact, a complicated process demanding not only a right spirit in men but qualities of organisation, energy, imagination and sacrifice and, above all, a long haul to see it through. We shall try to see in this closing chapter what this sustained effort to build a peaceful world, requires in practical terms, first from governments, then from the voluntary movements in which individuals combine for the pursuit of peace, and finally from the individual himself.

'We, the Peoples'

We have headed this chapter *Peoples and Peace*. The Charter of the United Nations which is an association of nation-states and in effect of governments, speaks of 'We, the Peoples', in whose name the obligations of the Charter are said to be undertaken. Governments in both their national and inter-national policies claim, with varying degrees of justification, to act on behalf of the peoples they represent. Voluntary movements and organisations are made up of people and depend by definition, on the willingness of people to cooperate in the pursuit of declared ends. Not only in this sense but in the more fundamental sense that all ideas and actions derive in the final analysis from individuals, people we can truly say, are the key to the processes and the prospects of peace.

What then can people do, first, through governments and by influence on governments, to advance the cause of peace

Witness for Peace at Westminster Abbey

and encourage the realisation of a warless world? Under dictatorial systems of government they can do little; their leaders are responsible effectively only to themselves. The question at the head of this paragraph is only relevant, therefore, where governments are elected by a truly democratic process and the peoples have the possibility of influencing the actions taken in their name. All the states-members of the United Nations have contracted in the Charter, except when confronted by direct attack, to abandon the use of force as an instrument of national policy and to settle their disputes by peaceful means. Yet four of the great powers within the United Nations can be said to have broken this pledge: Britain and France by their invasion of Egypt at the time of the Suez Canal crisis; the United States by warlike action in Vietnam and the Dominican Republic; the Soviet Union by its action in Hungary in 1956, and in Czechoslovakia in 1968. Some of the smaller member-states have also been involved in these contraventions of the Charter.

Pressure on governments

In all these instances, the countries concerned would claim justification for their actions by reference to some vital national or even international interest that had to be safeguarded. They would claim with some plausibility that until

the independence, or the security of nations, can be safeguarded by an effective system of international security
through the United Nations, nations must and will look after
their own security. Nevertheless the fact is that there will be no
real security and no assured peace for anyone, unless and until
great and small countries alike make the building of an
effective world security system and the general strengthening
of the United Nations, a first objective of their national policy.
Until they do this, the prime responsibility of their peoples is
to demand that this is accepted by their governments as a
supreme national and international interest.

The United Nations exists however, as we have acknowledged, not only to stop the use of armed force as an instrument
of national policy but to create the conditions of social justice
that will make a true and enduring peace possible. Member-
governments are also required to make available the material
resources which will enable the United Nations to carry out
its vital social and humanitarian tasks. The obligation is
accepted by most, if not all, the 'advanced' countries who must
provide the bulk of the aid the needy countries and peoples
require. Their governments tend to claim that they are doing
all that they can afford to do in financial and economic terms
to fulfil this commitment. The fact is, as we saw in Chapter
Three, that the aid they provide is in most cases only a tiny
percentage of their total wealth and much of it is not given but
lent. The business of governments who take seriously their
social obligations under the United Nations Charter and
correctly measure the gravity of the world poverty crisis, is
not only to increase their financial aid to the developing
countries but to enable these countries to have a greater share
in the volume of world trade. The business of those of their
citizens who want effective world action for peace and social
justice, is not only to provide public support for these policies
but to make clear their readiness to accept, if need be, some
reduction in their own high standards of living for the sake of
the under-privileged two-thirds of the world's peoples.

The truth is that most, if not all, the governments of the
member-states of the United Nations could do more to fulfil
the claim they frequently make that support for the United

Nations is the corner-stone of their foreign policy. The Government of the United Kingdom is no exception to this general rule. But in some degree the British Government has shown the way to the up-grading of the United Nations in official estimation and in the place given to it in foreign policy. The Permanent Delegate of the United Kingdom at the United Nations in recent years has been not, as formerly, a civil servant but a Minister of State in the Foreign Office, a member that is to say of the Government of the day and therefore carrying a direct share of responsibility for the Government's policies and actions. The process could be carried further but so far the trend is encouraging.

The peace movement

So much for the peace-making responsibilities of governments and the part the citizen can play in ensuring that they are accepted and fulfilled. What part is played and can be played through the unofficial, voluntary organisations in which for nearly two centuries citizens have combined to promote peace and international friendship and to bring pressure on their governments for these ends? The organised peace movement—to use a phrase now much less in vogue—can be said to have begun with the founding in 1816, at the instance of William Allen, an English Quaker, of the Society for Permanent and Universal Peace. The Society was British in origin and located in London but it was the forerunner of similar Peace Societies soon to be established in the United States and most of the countries of Western Europe and, later in the century, to be coordinated in the International Peace Bureau, with headquarters first in Berne and then in Geneva.

This was in no sense, and made no claim to be, a popular peace movement. Its participants, most of them men and women of some eminence in the intellectual and political life of their countries, came together in their International Peace Congresses (the first was held in London in 1843) which usually met in the Parliament buildings of Western capitals. There the delegates surveyed the world scene, appealed to rulers and statesmen to pursue policies of peace and made the practice of conveying their formal addresses and petitions in person to such crowned heads of Europe as were willing to receive them. This nineteenth-century peace movement had scarcely any influence on the course of world events or the succession of wars which punctuated the second half of the century, but it helped to popularise the concept of the settlement of international disputes through arbitration which dominated the proceedings of the Hague Conferences referred to in Chapter Six, and it laid the foundations for the larger and more popular movements that were to follow.

In the first quarter of the twentieth century, the accelerating race in naval armaments, the growing threat of a world war, and the war itself when it came in 1914, brought into being new organisations, essentially educational in character, and more amply supplied with financial and other resources. 1910 saw the setting-up in the United States, of the Carnegie Endowment for International Peace, financed by gifts from Andrew Carnegie, the American steel magnate, whose operations were later to become world-wide. The war years themselves brought to birth the Councils for International Friendship through the Churches, the Women's International League for Peace and Freedom—long to be the focus of the notable work of women and women's organisations in the cause of peace—and in Britain, the Union of Democratic Control which, stressing the dangers of secret treaties between rulers, sought to ensure that the momentous issues of war and peace were subject to the open and democratic discussion and decision of elected Parliaments. The founding of the League of Nations in 1919 prompted the setting up of League of Nations Societies—known in Britain as the League of Nations Union—in most of the countries in membership of the League, with the purpose of organising public support for the aims and activities of the world organisation.

The years between the two world wars saw two significant changes in the character and composition of this peace movement. The growth of Fascism in Europe under Hitler and Mussolini, and the menace of Japanese militarism in Asia, induced communist parties throughout the world to put themselves at the head of a so-called Popular Front against War and Fascism, for whose ends they sought to use the established and traditional peace organisations of the Western world. Determined resistance to the growth of Fascism was a respectable aim and could be claimed to be essential to the prevention of a Second World War. But the communists brought to their movement a temper and a propaganda more conducive to war than to peace, and the alliance with the other peace organisations was neither comfortable nor productive.

The spread of pacifism

Meanwhile, there had been a notable growth especially in the United States and Britain, of pacifist sentiment and of organisations bringing together those whose opposition to war, whether on religious or political grounds, was total and unconditional. Minority pacifist movements which owed much of their inspiration to the principles of non-violent resistance to evil and tyranny advocated and practised by such men as Mohandas K. Gandhi, the Indian leader, were formed in all the major religious denominations in Britain, America and elsewhere. An international organisation of War Resisters who refused on religious or political grounds to be conscripted for war, was established with headquarters in London. In 1934, the much-loved and respected 'Dick' Sheppard, later to become Canon of St. Paul's, founded his Peace Pledge Union, whose members pledged themselves to renounce war and to refuse support for any future war that might occur. The pacifists were still only a tiny minority of the Western communities in which they mainly flourished, but they made a much greater impact on the public mind in Britain at this time than the peace movements of the past and by 1939, the Peace Pledge Union could claim about one hundred and thirty-six thousand signatories to its pledge.

All these organisations survived the Second World War they had failed to prevent, though in the main with diminished strength. The United Nations Associations replaced the League of Nations Societies across the world, maintaining for the new world organisation, the broadly educational functions they had performed for the old. A new emphasis on the application of the federal principle, as seen in the federated United States of America, to international organisation, which aimed to create a United States of Europe and eventually a United States of the world—a World Government no less—brought into being Federal Union movements in Britain, in Western Europe, and in North America. The pre-war popular front of the communists re-emerged in the World Council of Peace which, like the popular front, was to all intents and purposes the mouthpiece of the foreign policy of the government of the Soviet Union.

The nuclear impact
It took several years, and the development of the atom bomb into the hydrogen bomb, for the discovery of nuclear weapons and the threat they presented to world peace and world survival, to make its full impact on the public mind. Once it was made, the major initiatives in popular action for peace passed from the traditional peace organisations with their general objectives, their sectional divisions and their very limited membership, to the more loosely-organised demonstration and protest movements whose slogan was 'BAN THE BOMB' and whose political purpose, in countries possessing nuclear weapons, was to persuade their government to renounce these weapons unilaterally—that is without reference to what other governments might or might not do. From 1951 onwards, various abortive attempts were made in Britain to establish a mass organisation committed to these aims but it was not until 1958 that the most influential and long-lasting of them all—the Campaign for Nuclear Disarmament (C.N.D.)—came into being. A few months earlier, a National Committee for a Sane Nuclear Policy had been set up in the United States with similar aims to Britain's C.N.D. and from 1959 onwards, C.N.D. movements arose in almost every West European country and in Canada, Australia and New Zealand.

In Britain, the Campaign for Nuclear Disarmament with its succession of Easter marches, often many thousands strong, from the nuclear weapons research centre at Aldermaston in Berkshire to central London, its mass rallies in Trafalgar Square, its 'ban the bomb' posters and button-hole badges, caught the imagination and dedicated support, especially, of the younger generation. Until its influence began to wane seven years later, C.N.D. secured for the 'peace movement' a degree of public attention it had never known before, and may never again acquire, in the same way. The idea of demonstrating publicly for peace passed to movements for peace in Vietnam in which genuine aspirations for a peaceful world and peaceful methods of attaining it, were confused with undisguised political aims focused largely on animosity to the United States, and a new note of violence crept into public witness for 'peace'.

The Campaign for Nuclear Disarmament achieved little that was concrete in political terms. It can claim that it encouraged the governments to make the Treaty which stopped most—though not all—testing of nuclear weapons, but it would be difficult to prove that, even here, its influence was a decisive factor. It persuaded the annual Conference of the British Labour Party, meeting at Scarborough in 1960, to vote for its policy of one-sided disarmament by Britain, but the vote was decisively reversed a year later at Blackpool. The Bomb was not banned and remains un-banned to the present day. The Campaign did, nevertheless, rouse public opinion on the moral issues raised by the possession and possible use of nuclear weapons; it gave some expression to the moral revulsion felt by millions of people—and not least the young— at the prospect of nuclear warfare; it gave to many a measure of relief from the sense of frustration and powerlessness which they felt in face of the looming menace of the Bomb.

Service for peace
One other latter-day development in the efforts of unofficial voluntary organisations to encourage international cooperation and the building of a peaceful world, remains to be mentioned. Between the two world wars, Pierre Ceresole, a Swiss pacifist, wanting to take practical steps to promote international reconciliation and seeking opportunities of constructive alternative service for Swiss citizens objecting on conscientious grounds to military service, founded his Service Civil International (S.C.I.). Members of S.C.I. joined with peoples of many nationalities in projects of reconstruction

and reclamation, in areas hit by natural calamities or disasters, where the people needed assistance and relief. Out of Pierre Ceresole's vision and idea can be said to have grown the whole movement of voluntary service for peace which today finds expression governmentally or inter-governmentally, in the technical assistance programmes of the United Nations but more directly still in such unofficial or semi-official organisations as the Peace Corps in the United States, or Voluntary Service Overseas and the International Service of the United Nations Association in Great Britain, which enable students and other younger persons, to spend a year abroad, working on little more than subsistence level, to help meet urgent social needs in Asia, Africa or Latin America.

Tasks for the individual

So much for the network of voluntary, non-governmental organisations—much changed in character and wider in their scope from the 'peace movement' of the early twentieth century—which participate in a variety of ways in the search for world peace. What can we say, finally, of the role and the responsibility of the individual in this whole enterprise? Since neither governments, at least in democratic societies, nor voluntary organisations, can function without people and without reference to public opinion, we can formulate three tasks for the individual person, all of them related to the functioning of organisations, whether official or unofficial. First, through the exercise of the vote and through membership in a political party, a trade union or other appropriate organisation, the individual citizen, as we saw earlier, can secure from government the positive policies inside and outside the United Nations which are likely to make for peace. This may, where some particularly flagrant injustice exists and urgent action is needed, involve him properly in the political action which takes the form of protest demonstrations, but in democratic societies, protest in this sense has to be sparingly used to be effective. It has above all, if it is to serve genuinely peaceful ends, to be non-violent and within the law.

Secondly, through active support of such voluntary organisations as the United Nations Association and its

Council for Education in World Citizenship, and by enlarging through study and travel his own knowledge of other countries and peoples, the individual can further the work of public education in the ideas and ideals of international cooperation and world citizenship which is necessary to the realisation of a peaceful world. Thirdly, he can, if he is young enough to do so, share, literally with his own hands, in practical tasks of peaceful service and reconstruction.

The heart of the matter

There is one additional word to be said about individual responsibility in the search for peace. In our opening chapter we spoke of the peaceable spirit as an essential element in the making of a peaceful international society. The peaceable spirit is required also in organisations and institutions but, at root, the peaceable spirit is a matter for the individual person. William Penn, whose 'Essay on the Future Peace of Europe' we noted in Chapter Seven, once said that 'those who would mend the world must first mend themselves.' George Fox told Cromwell's officers, who sought to enlist him in the civil war against Charles Stuart, that he lived 'in the virtue of that life and power that took away the occasion of all wars.' Penn and Fox were seventeenth-century Quakers, men of religious faith and conviction. Not all of us can use, or want to use, the religious terms which came naturally to them, but the truth of what they said remains. Peace has its roots and its ultimate strength in the mind and spirit of man. To quote UNESCO's constitution again: 'Since wars begin in the minds of men, it is in the minds of men that the defences of peace have to be constructed.' Peace cannot be guaranteed even to saints, or to the most enlightened of men, and there is no simple or automatic connection between the behaviour of individuals and the collective behaviour of groups and nations. But in achieving a loftier, more universal and more unselfish outlook and purpose for himself, the individual can and does set the pattern for the world he desires to create.

'No man' said John Donne, the sixteenth-century divine and poet, 'is an island, entire of itself. . . .' 'Any man's death', he went on to say, 'diminishes me because I am involved in mankind'. Albert Camus, the French writer who fought during the Second World War in the French Resistance against Hitler, put the same truth in modern terms when he said (in 1946):

> We know today that there are no more islands, that frontiers are just lines on a map. We know that in a steadily accelerating world, where the Atlantic is crossed in less than a day and Moscow speaks to Washington in a few minutes, we are forced into fraternity—or complicity. The forties have taught us that an injury done to a student in Prague strikes down simultaneously a worker in Clichy, that blood shed on the banks of a Central European river brings a Texas farmer to spill his own blood in the Ardennes which he sees for the first time. There is no suffering, no torture anywhere in the world which does not affect our everyday lives.

Certainly, those who want to take peace-making seriously today, have to become 'involved in mankind.' They have to see that what is in the best interests of others is in their own best interests too. They have to see other individuals, the world over, if not as children of the same God, at least as members of the same human family, inhabiting a world which is, in a phrase of U Thant's, 'an indivisible entity.' The alternatives, after all, are stark and simple enough. We have this vision of one world and make it a reality progressively, or we perish.

TOPICS FOR DISCUSSION

- Is it true that the 'war system' is the basis of modern society, which would fall apart without the 'cement' the system provides?

- In a warless world, how are we to absorb and use the energies and enthusiasms which war has absorbed in the past and to provide the excitement and adventure which has often been associated with the exploits of war?

- What kind of popular action by groups and individual persons is likely to be most effective in promoting peace today?

Suggested further reading

* denotes books for more advanced reading, or reference

CHAPTERS ONE AND TEN
War and Peace. Dominique Pire (Corgi, 1966)
Is Peace Possible? Kathleen Lonsdale (Penguin, 1957)
* *The Power of Non-Violence.* Richard B. Gregg (Clarke, 1959)
* *Voices from the Crowd—Against the H-Bomb.* Edited by David Boulton (Peter Owen, 1964)

CHAPTER TWO
A Policy for Disarmament. United Nations Association (London, 1965)
Must the Bomb Spread? Leonard Beaton (Penguin, 1966)
* *First Steps to Disarmament.* Edited by Evan Luard (Thames & Hudson, 1965)
* *Chemical and Biological Weapons.* U.N. Experts' Report (H.M.S.O., 1969)

CHAPTER THREE
Rich World/Poor World. Edited by James Lambe (Arrow Books, 1967)
* *World Poverty and British Responsibility.* Report commended by the British Council of Churches (S.C.M. Press, 1966)

CHAPTER FOUR
The U.N. and Southern Africa. U.N.A. (London, 1967)
* *The Future of South Africa.* Report for the British Council of Churches (S.C.M. Press, 1966)
* *Apartheid : its effect on Education, Science, Culture.* (Unesco, 1967)

CHAPTER FIVE
The USSR. Wright Miller (Oxford Press, 1967)
Soviet Russia. John Lawrence (Benn, 1967)

* *Survey of Russian History*. B. H. Sumner (Buckworth, 1961)
* *A Short History of Russia*. D. M. Sturley (Longmans, 1964)

CHAPTER SIX

China: Mao's Last Leap. Emily Macfarquhar (*The Economist*, 1968)
A Quarter of Mankind—An Anatomy of China Today. Dick Wilson (Penguin, 1968)
* *China: Yellow Peril? Red Hope?* C. R. Hensman (S.C.M. Press, 1968)
* *The Birth of Communist China*. C. P. Fitzgerald (Pelican, 1964)

CHAPTER SEVEN

Men against War. Nicholas Gillett (Gollancz, 1965)
* *A Great Experiment (The League of Nations)*, Lord Cecil (Cape, 1941)
* *The History of Peace*. A. C. F. Beales (Bell, 1931)

CHAPTERS EIGHT AND NINE

The Peacekeeping Experiment. Frances Boyd U.N.A. London, 1968)
The United Nations Family—The Work of the Specialised Agencies. Leslie R. Aldous (U.N.A. London, 1968)
* *The United Nations—A short political guide*. Sydney Bailey (Pall Mall, 1963)
* *Peace in the Family of Man*. Lester Pearson (B.B.C., 1969)
* *Everyman's United Nations*. (United Nations, 1968)

Illustrated brochures and booklets on all aspects of the work of the United Nations can be obtained from the UN Information Centres in London and many other capital cities.

Index